Virginia Woolf
&
the Raverats

A DIFFERENT SORT OF FRIENDSHIP

But there are very few people to whom one can write
good letters because they somehow don't react in the right
way, even if you like them (the people) quite well when
they are there. Perhaps it's a different sort of friendship.

Jaques Raverat, in a letter to Virginia Woolf

Virginia Woolf
&
the Raverats

A DIFFERENT SORT OF FRIENDSHIP

Edited by
WILLIAM PRYOR

CLEAR BOOKS

BATH

First published in Great Britain in 2003 by
Clear Books
Unit 136, 3 Edgar Buildings, George Street
Bath BA1 2FJ

www.clearpress.co.uk

© 2003 Clear Press Ltd

Letters, other writings, paintings, wood engravings & drawings
by Gwen & Jacques Raverat © 2003 Elisabeth Hambro
& Sophie Gurney

Virginia Woolf's letters & diary entries © 2003 Anne Olivier Bell
& Angelica Garnett

A CIP catalogue record for this title is
available from the British Library

ISBN 1 904555 02 0

Designed by Humphrey Stone

Bound & Printed in India by
Gopsons Papers Ltd.

Contents

Glossary of People & Places

Abbreviations: VB, Vanessa Bell; GR, Gwen Raverat; JR, Jacques Raverat; LW, Leonard Woolf; VW, Virginia Woolf.

THE APOSTLES, a select, mostly gay, Cambridge University club for the discussion of serious questions, founded late 1820s. Many male members of Bloomsbury were Apostles at the same time as VW's brother Thoby.

THE ADELPHI, a monthly magazine first published by John Middleton Murry in 1923 after his wife, Katherine Mansfield's death.

VON ANREP, Boris (1883–1969), Russian mosaicist, exhibited at Roger Fry's 2nd Post-Impressionist Exhibition in 1912; married Helen Maitland in 1918.

ARNOLD-FORSTER, Katherine, née Cox ('Ka' 1887–1938), a friend of VW, GR & JR, she married Will Arnold-Forster in 1918.

ARNOLD-FORSTER, Will (1885–1951), a painter, also worked for the Labour Party Committee on International Affairs, of which LW was Secretary.

ASHEHAM, house near Firle, Sussex that VW and VB leased in October 1911 and where LW and VW spent the first night of their honeymoon.

BELL, Clive (1881–1964), art critic, married Vanessa Stephen in 1907. Friend of VW's brother Thoby at Cambridge and lover of Mary Hutchinson.

BELL, Vanessa, née Stephen (1879–1961), painter, VW's sister, married Clive Bell in 1907, but from 1914 was the partner of Duncan Grant.

BENSON, Stella (1892–1933), suffragist and novelist who died in China.

BLOOMSBURY (Group), those English writers and artists who, between 1907 and 1930, would often meet at the houses of VW and VB in the Bloomsbury district of London near the British Museum.

BONNARD, Pierre (1867–1947), painter and printmaker, a recorder of France's *belle époque* and leading *colouriste*.

BRENAN, Gerald (1894–1987), son of an army officer, who once set off to walk to China; friend of Ralph Partridge and hence Carrington, with whom he was obsessed for years. Went to Spain to 'learn to write'.

BROOKE, Rupert (1887–1915), a poet, well-born, gifted and beautiful, whose early death in WWI helped turn him into a myth. VW labelled his admirers 'Neo-Pagans'; best-known work the sonnet sequence *1914*; died of septicaemia from a mosquito bite in Greece; buried in an olive grove on Skyros.

BRUYÉRE, Jean de la (1645–1696), French satirical moralist best known for one work, *Les Caractères de Théophraste.*

CARRINGTON, Dora (1893–1932), painter, known simply as 'Carrington'. Loved by Mark Gertler, she later set up house with Lytton Strachey and Ralph Partridge, whom she also adored and later married.

CHARLESTON FARMHOUSE, discovered by LW in May, 1916, became home to VB's menage (Duncan Grant & Bunny Garnet) until she died in 1961. Its quintessential Bloomsbury decorations and sculptures have since made it a superb museum.

CORNFORD, Frances, née Darwin (1886–1960), GR's first cousin, a poet, she suffered throughout her life from depression. Her *Collected Poems* appeared in 1954; awarded the Queen's Medal for Poetry in 1959.

CORNFORD, Francis (1890–1943), married Frances Darwin in 1909, classical scholar and friend of Jane Harrison.

CUNARD, Nancy (1896–1965), of the shipping family, an icon of twenties rebellious glamour, her long affair with a black man shocked her family. A poet, she founded the *Hours Press.*

DARWIN, Bernard (1876–1961), GR's cousin married Eily Monsell in 1906; famous as *The Times'* Golf Correspondent.

DARWIN, Billy (1894–1970), GR's youngest brother, a stockbroker.

DARWIN, Charles (1887–1962), a physicist, GR's younger brother lived at Newnham Grange after his mother's death in 1947.

DARWIN, Charles Robert (1809–1882), the evolutionist, GR's grandfather.

DARWIN, Eily, née Monsell (d. 1954), VW's 'pre-Bloomsbury' friend. After her marriage to Bernard Darwin, she encouraged GR to start wood engraving.

DARWIN, Lady Maud, née Du Puy (1861–1947), GR's mother was born in Pennsylvania and arrived in Cambridge in 1883, where she later became a formidable institution, as described in GR's *Period Piece.*

DARWIN, Sir George (1845–1912), GR's father, though shaded by his father's brilliance, became Plumian Professor of Astronomy and Experimental Philosophy at Cambridge. He married Maud Du Puy in 1884.

FRY, Roger (1866–1934), Apostle, art critic, painter and core Bloomsburyite, introduced Post-Impressionism to Britain & founded the Omega Workshop.

GIDE, André (1869–1951), writer who received the Nobel Prize for Literature in 1947. He befriended JR at Paul Desjardines' *entretiens*, or summer school, at Pontigny. They remained close friends for the rest of JR's life.

GILL, Eric (1882–1940), sculptor, engraver, typographer, especially known for his elegant typefaces; he made the relief *Prospero and Ariel* over the entrance of Broadcasting House, London; a friend of GR & JR.

GIRADOUX, Jean (1882–1944), French novelist and playwright who created impressionistic drama by emphasizing dialogue and style over realism.

GORDON SQUARE, Bloomsbury, VB rented No 46 in October 1904 which remained one of the centres of Bloomsbury for the next three decades.

GRANT, Duncan (1885–1978), painter, lived & worked with VB from 1914 till her death in 1961; their daughter, Angelica was born in 1918.

HARRISON, Jane (1850–1928), distinguished classical scholar at Newnham College, Cambridge. Her student, Hope Mirrlees, became her 'ghostly daughter' and companion when they moved to Paris.

HAM SPRAY, near Hungerford on the Thames, the house Lytton Strachey moved into in 1924 with Carrington and Ralph Partridge.

THE HERETICS, Cambridge University discussion group founded in 1911.

HOGARTH HOUSE in Richmond, Surrey, leased by VW and LW in 1915.

HOGARTH PRESS was started in the cellar of Hogarth House by LW and VW in 1917, in part as physical therapy for VW.

HUTCHINSON, Mary, née Barns (1889–1977), first cousin once removed of Lytton Strachey, married to a barrister, for thirteen years Clive Bell's lover.

KEYNES, Geoffrey (1887–1982), surgeon, bibliographer and Blake scholar, brother of Maynard.

KEYNES, Margaret, née Darwin (1890–1975), GR's sister, who married Geoffrey Keynes.

KEYNES, Maynard (1883–1946), brother of Geoffrey, economist, journalist, and financier, Apostle at King's College, Cambridge; married ballerina Lydia Lopokova in 1925. In 1923 become chairman of the Board of *the Nation & the Athenaeum* and appointed Leonard Woolf literary editor.

KINGLAKE, Alexander (1809–1891), early travel writer admired by VW (and Winston Churchill), for his *Eothen: Traces of Travel Brought Home from the East*.

LITCHFIELD, Mrs Henrietta, née Darwin, ('Aunt Etty' 1843–1927) GR's aunt.

LITTLE TALLAND HOUSE, VW's first house in Sussex.

LOPOKOVA, Lydia (1892–1981), Russian ballerina, studied at the Imperial School of Ballet, St Petersburg, danced with Diaghilev's *Ballet Russe* and married Maynard Keynes in 1925.

MANOR FARM, Croydon, 15 miles south west of Cambridge, where GR and JR lived from 1912 until 1915.

MANSFIELD, Katherine, adopted name of the New Zealand-born writer Kathleen Mansfield Beauchamp (1888–1923), married John Middleton Murry in 1918. Though VW felt competitive with her, her long short story *Prelude* (1918) was the third publication of the Hogarth Press. She died at the Gurdjieff Institute in Switzerland.

MARCHAND, Jean (1883–1931), painter and printmaker who lived near Vence, his work was admired by Roger Fry. He became close friends with both GR and JR. He had a short-lived affair with GR after JR's death.

MIDDLETON MURRY, John (1889–1957), literary critic, editor and author, married Katherine Mansfield in 1918.

MIRRLEES, Hope (1887–1978), poet, novelist and translator, a pupil of Jane Harrison at Newnham College, Cambridge before going to live with her in Paris. Her publications include: *Paris: A Poem*, Hogarth Press 1920, *The Life of Archpriest Avvakam by Himself*, translated by Jane Harrison and Hope Mirrlees, Hogarth Press, 1924, and *Lud-in-the-Mist*, a surrealist novel that had a surprise life as a precursor of the Fantasy genre when re-published in the 1970's.

MONKS HOUSE, near Rodmell in Sussex, which the Woolfs bought in 1919.

MORELL, Lady Ottoline, née Cavendish-Bentinck (1873–1938), half-sister of the 6th Duke of Portland, was a famous hostess of parties for writers, artists and politicians at her Oxfordshire house, Garsington.

THE NATION, a weekly literary magazine that published most of Bloomsbury at one time or another. As its Chairman, Maynard Keynes offered LW the literary editorship in 1923. In 1921 it had absorbed Middleton Murry's *Athanaeum* and was itself merged with the *New Statesman* in 1931.

NEO-PAGANS, the name VW (in part to distance herself from it) gave the group that gravitated towards Rupert Brooke in the 1900s and 1910s. Their Edwardian back-to-nature, almost hippy, inclinations were expressed in cross-country treks, skinny-dipping, Fabianism and endless late-night discussions about serious artistic and social issues.

Through their friendship with Brooke, both GR and JR were considered Neo-Pagan.

NEWNHAM GRANGE, the Cambridge house where GR was born, bought by her father, George Darwin, in 1885. A branch of the River Cam runs through its grounds which also incorporate the Old Granary where GR wrote *Period Piece* and died in 1957. The whole complex now forms the core of Darwin College. The Blue Plaque for GR on the Silver Street entrance was the first for a woman in Cambridge.

NICOLSON, Harold (1886–1968), diplomat and author, son of 1st Baron Carnock, married Vita Sackville-West in 1913. A prolific author of 125 books, he retired from the diplomatic service in 1929.

THE OLD GRANARY, Cambridge, part of Newnham Grange, next to Silver Street Bridge and GR's home for the last ten years of her life.

PÉGUY, Charles (1873–1914), French poet & philosopher, killed in WWI, who combined Christianity, socialism, & patriotism into his faith.

PRUNOY, Chateau de Vienne, Georges Raverat's country house near Orléans.

PRYOR, Mark (1915–1970), married to Sophie Raverat in 1940, an entomologist and Senior Tutor at Trinity College, Cambridge. His parents rented the Raverats a house in Hertfordshire during WWI.

PRYOR, William (b.1945), erstwhile neoDadaist and beatnik, son of Sophie and Mark Pryor, grandson of Gwen and Jacques Raverat, editor of this book.

RADIGUET, Raymond (1903–1923), precocious French writer and poet, a Dadaist and Cubist protégé of Jean Cocteau at the age of 16. Apollinaire teased him: 'Don't despair; Monsieur Rimbaud waited until he was seventeen before writing his masterpiece'. Died aged just 20.

RAVERAT, Elisabeth (b.1916), eldest daughter of the Raverats, in 1940 married Edvard Hambro, diplomat and son of the Speaker of the Norwegian Parliament, who helped the government escape the Nazis into exile.

RAVERAT, Georges (1860–1938), father of JR, a successful entrepreneur, burgher of Le Havre and, unusually for a Frenchman, a vegetarian.

RAVERAT, Gwendolen née Darwin ('Gwen' 1885–1957), eldest child of George and Maud Darwin, born at Newnham Grange, studied at the Slade School of Art, a childhood friend of VB and VW, married JR in 1911 and moved to France with him in 1920. After his death she returned to London in 1925, illustrated many books, becoming a leading wood engraving artist of the 20th century. In 1930, at the suggestion of her brother-in-law, Geoffrey Keynes, she designed the sets and costumes for the Sadler's Wells ballet, *Job, A Masque for Dancing*, with music by her cousin Ralph Vaughan Williams (also a cousin of VW). In 1949 she started work on *Period Piece*, which was published in 1952 and is still in print.

RAVERAT, Sophie (b. 1919), youngest daughter of the Raverats, married Mark Pryor in 1940.

RYLANDS, George ('Dadie' 1902–1991), educated at Eton and King's College, Cambridge, where he became an Apostle. After assisting VW and LW with Hogarth Press he returned to King's to teach English.

SACKVILLE-WEST, The Hon. Edward ('Eddie' 1901–1965), son and heir of the 4th Baron Sackville and Vita's cousin.

SACKVILLE-WEST, Victoria ('Vita' 1892–1962), novelist and poet, VW's lover and only child of Lionel Edward, 3rd Baron Sackville, and Victoria Josepha Dolores Catalina Sackville-West, the Baron's first cousin, married Harold Nicolson in 1913. The Hogarth Press published thirteen of her books.

SEGONZAC, André Dunoyer de (1884–1974), French painter and printmaker.

SHOVE, Fredegund, née Maitland (1889–1949), daughter of VW's cousin Florence (Fisher) and the historian F. W. Maitland, married Gerald Shove (1887–1947), economist, Fellow of King's College Cambridge and an Apostle. In 1922 the Hogarth Press published Fredegund's poems, *Daybreak*.

SICKERT, Walter (1860–1942), painter and printmaker, the most important of the English Impressionists.

SITWELL, Edith (1887–1964), English poet who first gained fame for her stylistic artifices but who emerged during World War II as a poet, famed for her formidable personality, Elizabethan dress, and eccentric opinions.

SITWELL, Sir Osbert, 5th Baronet (1892–1969), man of letters who became famous, with his sister Edith, as a tilter at establishment windmills in literature and the arts.

THE SLADE SCHOOL OF FINE ART opened as part of University College, London in 1870. Students relevant to this book include Augustus & Gwen John, Wyndham Lewis, Stanley Spencer, GR, Mark Gertler, Dora Carrington, Sophie Raverat, Paul Nash and Ben Nicholson, while Roger Fry taught art history there.

SPENCER, Stanley (1891–1959), leading 20th-century English painter, whose work has a strange religiosity, surrealist overtones, a curiously distorted style of drawing, and a strong element of satirical social comment. His close friendship with GR, sustained until her death, started at the Slade, when she supported him by buying his work.

STEPHEN, Adrian (1883–1948), VW's younger brother, with whom she lived at 29 Fitzroy Square after VB's marriage in 1907, and who, like his wife Karin, became a psychoanalyst.

STEPHEN, Karin, née Costelloe (1889–1953), stepdaughter of Bernard Berenson, niece of Logan Pearsall Smith and of Bertrand Russell's first wife Alys, married Adrian Stephen.

STEPHEN, Sir Leslie (1832–1904), VW's father, critic, man of letters, and first editor of the *Dictionary of National Biography.*

STEPHEN, Thoby (1880–1906), VW's brother, an Apostle at Cambridge, several of whose friends joined Bloomsbury. He died of typhoid aged 26.

STRACHEY, Lytton (1880–1932), critic & biographer, a friend of both Thoby Stephen & LW at Trinity College, Cambridge & also an Apostle. After her brother's death in 1906, Lytton became one of VW's close friends and briefly contemplated marrying her. His best-known work, *Eminent Victorians,* was published in 1918. Later he lived with Carrington and Ralph Partridge at Ham Spray House, Hungerford.

SYDNEY-TURNER, Saxon (1880–1962), a civil servant, Apostle and close friend of Thoby Stephen, LW and Lytton Strachey at Cambridge.

TIME & TIDE, the magazine founded in 1920 by VW's friend Lady Margaret Rhondda, who employed GR as resident artist from 1927 and later as art critic. Contributors to the magazine included D. H. Lawrence, Vera Brittain, VW and LW, Nancy Astor, Emmeline Pankhurst, Olive Schreiner, Rebecca West, Rose Macaulay, Naomi Mitchison, Ethel Smyth, George Bernard Shaw, Robert Graves and George Orwell. *Time and Tide* never sold well and it is estimated that the magazine lost Lady Rhondda over £500,000 during the 38 years she owned it. It folded in 1977.

TREFUSIS, Violet, née Keppel (1894–1972), Camilla Parker-Bowles's great aunt and eldest daughter of Alice Keppel, Edward VII's mistress. Her affair with Vita Sackville-West, after she had married Denys Trefusis, an officer in the Royal Horse Guards, culminated in 1920 in the women running away to Amiens in France. The husbands flew there in a private plane to bring them home.

13

TURNER, Percy, JR's gallery at 7a Grafton Street, London.

VALÉRY, Paul (1871–1945), French poet, essayist, and critic. A national literary figure by the 1920s, his friendship with André Gide led him to meet JR at Prunoy and visit him at Vence.

VILLA ADÈLE, the house near Vence in the south of France, that GR and JR lived in from 1920 to 1925 and where JR died.

WOOLF, Leonard (1880–1969), man of letters, publisher, political worker, journalist, and internationalist, married VW in 1912. After her death he acted as her archivist.

WOOLF, Virginia, née Stephen (1882–1941), writer and critic.

Jacques Raverat as a Bedales schoolboy c. 1901

14

Introduction

The central fact of this book is the death, on March 7th, 1925, of my grandfather, Jacques Raverat, aged just 40, from multiple sclerosis. Central because, from 1922, the book's three protagonists: Virginia Woolf, Jacques and his wife Gwen, must have all known his death was inevitable, unavoidable. Death hovers around everything they write to each other, if not on the surface, then close to it.

In a letter written in 1919 Virginia Woolf says she 'always had a deep affection for' Jacques. And though Gwen plays her diffident part, the crucial bond was that between Jacques and Virginia. This meeting of spirits would find its apotheosis in the letters they exchanged after the Raverats' move to France had put geographical distance between them.

My grandmother, Gwen Raverat, née Darwin, granddaughter of the evolutionist, survived Jacques for 32 fruitful years. After his death, she moved back to England, first London then Cambridge, where her art focused on wood engraving, for which she became justifiably renowned. Only in her 64th year did she start work on *Period Piece*, the best-selling memoir of her childhood that has been in print continuously since its publication in 1952.

Gwen's father, Sir George Darwin, and Virginia's father, Sir Leslie Stephen, were good friends – their families, prominent in British intelligentsia, moved in the same rarified academic circles. Virginia would visit the Darwin home, Newnham Grange, when in Cambridge to see her brother Thoby, who was up at Trinity. When he died of typhoid in 1906, Gwen was shocked. She wrote to her sister: 'The four Stephens . . . seemed built on a larger scale than most people; and their bodies matched their souls. And Thoby seemed biggest of all. It's something gone out of one's imagination.'

Virginia continued to visit the Darwins when in Cambridge. In an early and recently unearthed journal, we read her account, quoted in full on page 23, of a visit she made in 1909.

Jacques Raverat came from an unusual French family – his father, a rich entrepreneur from Le Havre was not only a vegetarian, but was attracted to the kind of education the newly developing English progressive schools like Bedales could offer. After Bedales, the Sorbonne and his military service, Jacques entered Emmanuel College, Cambridge, in October 1906, to read mathematics.

As soon as Jacques arrived in Cambridge, he gravitated towards an interesting group of bohemian spirits led by the poet Rupert Brooke with whom a close friendship blossomed. It was also soon after this that Jacques first noticed something strangely wrong with his health: unaccountable fatigue and unsteadiness on his legs. When his mother committed suicide at the end of that November he had to return to France, not able to finish even his first term.

In 1908, the Marlowe Dramatic Society, founded by

Rupert Brooke, put on a production of Milton's *Comus*. Gwen, Jacques (now returned to Cambridge), Gwen's cousin Frances Cornford and others, inspired by Rupert's magnetism, formed a loose group that Virginia would later label the 'Neo-Pagans'. By July 1908, Jacques' persistent ill health had forced him to abandon any hope of returning to the university. His doctor's advice to give up mathematics and take up a craft led to him first spending time as an art printer before becoming a painter.

In October 1908, Gwen started at the Slade School of Painting and Drawing in London. She saw more of the Stephen family, dining with Virginia and Adrian in Fitzroy Square and attending meetings of Vanessa's Friday Club, soon becoming its Secretary. Thus Gwen was both a Neo-Pagan and involved in the founding of what became the Bloomsbury Group.

After a somewhat tempestuous triangular affair involving Ka Cox – later to be an intimate of Virginia's – Jacques and Gwen were married in June, 1911. Not till 1914 was he diagnosed as having what was then called 'disseminated sclerosis'. They spent the war years rather isolated in England, Jacques feeling bitterly disappointed that his health prevented him going to the front. In 1920 they moved to Vence, in the south of France, for his health.

In 1922, after a silence of 10 years, Virginia and Jacques renewed their acquaintance by letter. They ranged far and wide: gossip, the nature of friendship, religion, the endurance of pain, the eccentric behaviour of Maynard Keynes's new ballerina love, Lydia Lopokova, Jacques's anti-semitism, Virginia's sapphism, the differences between painting and writing. Informed by the depressions and uncertainties, the speculation and passion of their bohemian lives, these letters display a complex affinity between three artists facing their own mortality, their weaknesses and the price of their creativity.

Virginia never sent anyone advance copies of her books, but in 1924, she sent Jacques, now very ill, a proof copy of *Mrs Dalloway*. The letter Jacques dictated to Gwen about the book gave Virginia, 'one of the happiest days of [her] life'.

For all but one of the letters, Gwen was Jacques' scribe (he was mostly too weak to hold a pen) enabling her to put herself in the conversation every now and then. The letters between the two women immediately after Jacques' death are some of the most moving.

Indeed, the only letter, of the many thousands Virginia wrote, to be quoted in the *Faber Book of Letters* was the first she wrote to Gwen after Jacques's death: *I go about thinking of you both, in starts, & almost constantly underneath everything, & I don't know what to say. One thing that comes over & over is the strange wish I have to go on telling Jacques things. This is for Jacques, I say to myself; I want to write to him about happiness, & about Rupert, & love.*

This is a friendship whose substance and passion was entirely expressed by letter. Several times Virginia made plans to visit the Raverats in France, plans that were always thwarted. Before the Raverats left for France they saw little of Virginia and wrote rarely; after Gwen's return to England and Virginia's help in finding her a job on the magazine *Time & Tide*, they saw each other rarely – though my mother does remember going to Charleston, Vanessa Bell's farmhouse in Sussex, for her daughter Angelica's 21st birthday party in 1940, a party at which Virginia sat regally and quietly in the corner.

It is striking how almost nervous – certainly self-conscious – the Raverats and Virginia are of each other. Both sides are somehow awed by reputations and mythologies they have come to believe. And yet the compassion Virginia feels for both Jacques and Gwen (despite her more testy remarks in letters to others and in her diary) is evident throughout; not in direct expression of sympathy or cloying pity, but in her preference to give his impending death meaning through the intensity with which she writes to him about living, art, friendship and even gossip.

While Jacques' most telling comment on his illness is to thank God for morphine, it is not until after his death that Gwen writes – and then most eloquently – about their suffering. Though she feels that 'certain things – horrors or intimacies or heroisms or madness – have to be written about with very great restraint else they get out of key' she manages to reach out to her friend Virginia from her suffering.

This book is the vapour trail left by a remarkable friendship, as they 'cantered out on paper', to use Virginia's phrase, a friendship that took all three of them beyond their usual confines.

WILLIAM PRYOR
Bath 2003

Note on the Presentation of the Letters

The layout of the letter headings and to a lesser extent
the dates and places from where the letters were written have been standardised. Otherwise the punctuation
and spelling of the letters are as they were written – with
the exception that the titles of books and magazines as
well as words underlined for emphasis by the authors
have been italicised.

England 1909 to 1920

sketch for a bookplate for Virginia Stephen, by Gwen Raverat

Since there was no 29th of February in 1909, this must have been written on March 1st, about a trip to Cambridge that included this visit to Newnham Grange, Gwen Darwin's family home. Virginia was 27 and working on her first novel, The Voyage Out. *Gwen was in her first year at the Slade School of Art. Jacques may have been in Florence studying art.*

29th February [1909]

The Darwins' house is a roomy house, built in the 18th century I suppose, overlooking a piece of green. The first things I saw, stepping in from the snow, were a wide hall, with a fire in the middle of it. It is altogether comfortable,

Newnham Grange from the River, by Gwen Raverat,
illustration for *Period Piece*, 1951

and homely. The ornaments, of course, are of the kind that one associates with Dons, and university culture. In the drawing room, the parents' room, there are prints from Holbein drawings, bad portraits of children, indiscriminate rugs, chairs, Venetian glass, Japanese embroideries: the effect is of subdued colour, and incoherence; there is no regular scheme. In short the room is dull.

The children's room revolts against the parents': they like white walls, modern posters, photographs from the old masters. If they could do away with the tradition, I imagine that they would have bare walls, and a stout table; with both ideals I find myself in opposition.

In truth the Darwin temperament deserves some discussion. The parents – Sir George alone was visible – are somewhat obliterated, of course; Sir George is now a very kindly ordinary man, with whom his children are entirely at their ease. It is strange that a man who must have known great men, and who is at work always upon great problems, should have nothing distinguished or remarkable about him. At first one is mildly relieved, and later, one is disappointed. His sensible and humorous remarks, his little anecdotes, and his shrewd judgments, are natural to him; no mask, as one had hoped. He is clearly affectionate, much interested in small events, and satisfied with his position. It is also clear that he has no feeling for beauty, no romance, or mystery in his mind; in short, he is a solid object, filling his place in the world, and all one may ever hope to find in him is a sane judgment, a cheerful temper. The liveliest thing about him is

Newnham Grange from Silver Street, by Gwen Raverat,
illustration for *Period Piece*, 1951

his affection for his children; he is inclined to be peppery,
likes punctuality, good manners and tidiness; lectured us,
for instance, upon the importance (often overlooked by
young ladies) of good shoes. He notices small things; and
that, at his age, gives him a certain charm. He is like some
elderly but wiry grey terrier, with short legs, and choleric
eyes, rather watering at the corners.

His wife (she was in bed) is a big sensible woman; with a
trace of American decision: but otherwise merely practical
and kindly: coarse I daresay in her view, if one got to know
her well. The children almost openly prefer their father.

The children are naturally more interesting. For at their
ages, 19 and 24, they are beginning to test their surround-
ings. [*Gwen, born in 1885, was in fact the oldest of five children: Charles, Margaret, Billy and Leonard who died as a baby*

25

Mill Lane (seen from the Old Granary, part of Newnham Grange), by Gwen Raverat, wood engraving (reduced in size), 1948

– the nineteen year old is Margaret who would later marry Geoffrey Keynes, brother of Maynard.] They are anxious to get rid of Darwin traditional culture and have a notion that there is a free Bohemian world in London, where exciting people live. This is all to their credit; and indeed they have a certain spirit which one admires. Somehow, however, it applies itself to the wrong things. They aim at beauty, and that requires the surest touch. Gwen tends (this is constructive criticism) to admire vigorous, able, sincere works, which are not beautiful; she attacks the problems of life in the same spirit; and will end in 10 years time by

being a strong and sensible woman, plainly clothed; with the works of deserving minor artists in her house. Margaret has not the charm which makes Gwen better than my account of her; a charm arising from the sweetness and competency of her character. She is the eldest of the family. Margaret is much less formed; but has the same determination to find out the truth for herself, and the same lack of any fine power of discrimination. They enjoy things very much, and fancy that this is due to their superior taste; fancy that in riding about the streets of Cambridge they are building up a theory of life. I think I find them content with what seems to me rather obvious; I distrust such violent discontent, and the easy remedies. But I admire much also: only find the Darwin temperament altogether too definite, burly, and industrious. They exhibit the English family life at its best; its humour, tolerance, heartiness, and sound affection.

Clare Bridge, by Gwen Raverat, wood engraving (reduced in size), 1935

TWO EXCERPTS FROM AN UNFINISHED NOVEL
BY GWEN RAVERAT

Rupert Brooke's death in 1915 from the septicaemia that developed from a mosquito bite brought an end to a vision and started a myth. The group that Virginia Woolf called the Neo-Pagans revolved around him and the Raverats' friendship with him meant they were tarred with that brush. In 1916 Gwen started a novel, set in 1906, about a group of young friends, centring around a charismatic figure she called Hubert. She never finished the book, though in these two excerpts she does manage to capture something of the bohemian adventure Rupert was taking them on. It is clear that Hubert is Rupert Brooke while George was based on Jacques.

These were friendships that changed our whole lives... We met, we found we had many ideas in common; we found that we could talk. And so we talked from morning to night and from night till morning, and for the first two years we did practically nothing else. We had been shy and diffident; we had wondered if anyone had ever had such ideas as ours before; we had wondered if they could possibly be true ideas; if there was the remotest chance that we could be worth anything. Now, when we came together many of our doubts disappeared; we were passionately convinced of the truth and splendour of our thoughts; we felt that we were quite different from our fathers; all our ways of thinking and our opinions seemed bold and new. And though each of us alone might still doubt his own powers, we each thought that never before

29

had there met together a group of such fine and intelligent young men. I think that we each thought ourselves singularly happy in having such wonderful friends.

From the beginning it was from Hubert that we expected great things; it was Hubert we all watched and loved. Perhaps the most obvious thing about him was his beauty. He was not so beautiful as many another man has been, and yet there was something in his appearance, which it was impossible to forget. It was no good laughing at him; calling him pink and white, or chubby; saying his eyes were too small or his legs too short. There was a nobility about the carriage of his head and the shape of it, a radiance in his fair hair and shining face, a sweetness and a secrecy in his deep set eyes, a straight strength in his limbs, which remained for ever in the minds of those who once had seen him; which penetrated and coloured every thought of him.

I remember those first two years as long days and nights of talk; talk, lying in the cow parsley under the great elms; talk in lazy punts on the river; talk round the fire in Hubert's room; talk which seemed always to get nearer and nearer to the heart of things. It was best of all in the evenings in Hubert's room. He used to lie in his great armchair, his legs stretched right across the floor, his fingers twisted in his hair; while George sat smoking by the fire, continually poking it; his face was round and pale; his hair was dark. We smoked and ate muffins or sweets and talked and talked while the firelight danced on the ceiling, and all the possibilities of the world seemed open to us.

For a time we were very decadent. We used to loll in armchairs and talk wearily about Art and Suicide and the Sex Problem. We used to discuss the ridiculous superstitions about God and Religion; the absurd prejudices of patriotism and decency; the grotesque encumbrances called parents. We were very, very old and we knew all about everything; but we often forgot our age and omniscience and played the fool like anyone else.

Long silences would fall upon us when we sat together thus; often we all went off into dreams of our own and forgot to talk; and the fire jumped and flickered, and the cabs rumbled outside.

And – I don't know what the others felt – but to my mind, always hidden among the shadows behind our backs, was Death – Death waiting to catch us who were so young and full of hope; Death, ready to snap us up before our work was done – Death, barely hidden, waiting to destroy all our youth and beauty and grace.

Jacques Raverat

Gwen Raverat

Virginia Woolf

Gwen and Jacques were engaged in February 1911. Virginia was working on The Voyage Out; *her heroine's question: 'Why do people marry?' reverberates through the book. Firle is a small village under the Sussex Downs near Lewes where Virginia rented a semidetached cottage which she called 'Little Talland House' after the family holiday home in Cornwall.*

29, Fitzroy Square, W.   [early 1911]

Dear Mr Raverat,

   On hearing of your important engagement, I was ready to let you off the other one. But Gwen says you will come, without cursing. The train is the 3.20 from Victoria on Saturday. We are going by that, so I hope you may be able to.

   My congratulations are very warm. As I said, I have heard so much of you, that I can congratulate her too.

   Yours
   Virginia Stephen

   It will probably be ghastly uncomfortable at Firle. Take a weekend ticket to Lewes.

Gwen met Jacques's father when she visited the Chateau de Vienne at Prunoy, the Raverat country house near Orléans, south of Paris, late in 1910. The original letter was in French.

Cambridge   2nd March 1911

... I would like to speak of her. I believe it's very true and fair to say that she is not 'sympathique'. The great spirits never are. She has a proud soul, very fierce and strong... She wants to write to you. That will begin it. She loves you very much (she had already told me that at Prunoy) and you will love her too; as one loves great things, Rembrandt or Shakespeare ...

I kiss you on the forehead between the eyes.

Don't be sad. I want it.

Yours, always, Jacques.

FROM VIRGINIA STEPHEN TO JACQUES RAVERAT

Little Talland House, Firle,
Lewes
Sussex   April 9th [1911]

Dear Jacques,

I've been long in writing, but I knew you would put that down to the infernal confusion of London – not to ingratitude. It was delightful of you to think of sending that book. In fact you have a delightful nature. Thank you so much. I've just been cutting the pages, & seeing several bold words which tempt me on, in spite of the Sabbath. I shall begin seriously after dinner.

We left London in a flurry, but now I'm here alone & shall be alone for a fortnight. I read furiously & write & walk. It's a very satisfactory life, & much more exciting, even than talking. As for the country, I never imagined anything so beautiful. I've discovered several new walks.

You & Gwen must come here again. By the way, would this house be any use to you both for a week or fortnight after the 23rd? I shall probably be in France with Ka; away anyhow; & it seems a pity that all these sights shouldn't be seen.

One can put up six, as you know.

Thank you again. Yours ever.

Virginia Stephen

I can't remember your address. I hope your walk was good.

Vanessa Bell, VW's sister was in Turkey, where she had a mis-cariage. Elinor ('Eily') Monsell, a young Irish artist friend of Virginia's, of considerable charm and wit, who had been at the Slade in 1896, married Gwen's cousin Bernard Darwin in 1906. It was her encouragement that inspired Gwen to become an artist. The 'large sum' that Virginia says Bernard earned for a 'story' would have been for his golf journalism for The Times. *Katherine ('Ka') Cox met Gwen and Jacques when at Newnham College. A kindly, dependable woman, she was to be a good friend of the Woolfs, particularly during Virginia's illnesses. In this letter to her sister, Virginia's account of the turbulent triangle between Ka, Gwen and Jacques, overstates, perhaps, Gwen's naïvety. Gwen and Jacques were married just 7 weeks after this letter was written on 7th June at Kensington Registry Office.*

Little Talland House, Firle,
Lewes, Sussex   19th April [1911]

Beloved,

I've just come in from meeting Eily, and find your wire. As you say all is well, I suppose I am a fool to worry. At any rate all my doubts will be cleared up tomorrow or Friday, so I wont waste paper describing them. Only if you knew what anxieties you can send across the ocean, you would be excessively careful. You seem to do so much; aren't your males a little exacting?

I've had some intercourse with the world since I wrote. Ka came striding along the road in time for lunch yester-

Ka Cox, charcoal, by Jacques Raverat
(sketched at Firle on the 5th of March, 1918)

day; with a knapsack on her back, a row of red beads, and daisies stuck in her coat. Her innocent face was brown. We went for a walk; and lay on the grass, and surveyed the view. Then she began to tell me of her private affairs, which are very private; so dont share them. What advice would you have given I wonder? The state of the case is this.

Jacques, as you know, proposed to her, less than a year ago. She refused him several times. At last this autumn, thinking she would never care, she urged him to consider Gwen. Gwen quickly fell in love; and Jacques, seeing this, was overcome, proposed, and was accepted. He says now that he is in love with them both; and asks Ka to be his mistress, and Gwen to satisfy his mind. Gwen is made very jealous; Ka evidently cares a good deal for Jacques. Obviously (in my view) J. is very much in love with K: and not much, if at all, with Gwen. Ought they to break off the engagement? J. has doubts, occasionally; Ka sometimes thinks she could marry him; Gwen alternately grows desperate, and then, accepting J's advanced views, suggests that Ka shall live with them, and bear children while she paints.

There are endless possibilities of discomfort; but cynically considering the infantile natures of all concerned, I predict nothing serious. Ka will marry a Brooke next year, I expect. J. will always be a Volatile Frog. Gwen will bear children, and paint pictures; clearly though, J. and K. would be the proper match.

I've just seen Ka off, and fetched Eily here. Eily is very stout; but very nice. In the pauses between raptures over hills and clouds, she gave me her version of the affair.

She agrees with me that J. is much more in love with K. than with Gwen; she thinks the risks tremendous; but says that if it is broken off, Gwen will certainly go off her head.

I rather doubt that; but she would be very unhappy and perhaps this is her only chance. The trouble is, to my mind, that they're none of them clever enough to carry the thing through successfully; and J. has muddied their minds with talk of the unchastity of chastity.

God! how I wish I knew about you! I am now going to take Eily for a walk. She has already told me that its a great bore marrying a man without taste. Having made a large sum by a story, Bernard [*Darwin*] bought her a picture, as a surprise; it was a work by a man called [*George*] Belcher, who draws for Punch. She says she found it very difficult to be grateful.

We shall go to France on Monday night, 24th. Address letters to Post Restante, Poitiers. until 31st. I shall come back on the 1st I think. All the places are close, so Poitiers will be our headquarters.

Yr. B. [*VW was a consumate inventer of nicknames – to Vanessa, Virginia was 'Billy Goat' or 'B.' for short.*]

The man at the post office has supplied me with this remarkable address.

Virginia and Leonard were married on 10th August 1912. They were sharing Asheham with her sister, Vanessa Bell. On 9th March 1913 Leonard delivered the typescript of The Voyage Out *to Virginia's half brother, Gerald Duckworth's publishing house. Gwen and Jacques were living in the isolated Manor Farm, Croydon, halfway between Cambridge and Biggleswade. Gwen was working on a three-foot-tall painting called* Two Women *which would be hung at the New English Art Club exhibition that May. Gwen's letter to which Virginia is replying is lost, but the insult and anger she refers to are to do with Rupert Brooke's emotional rejection of Bloomsbury and Virginia's antagonism towards Neo-Paganism. Gwen and Jacques had holidayed at Harbour View, Studland Bay in Dorset in January and February 1912.*

Asheham House,
Rodmell,
Lewes   Sunday [23rd March 1913]

Dear Gwen,

I didn't realise that you'd insulted me, or rather the people who live in London. Of course, your letters generally make me very angry, but that's because of the spirit of neo-paganism that breathes so fierce in them, & I'm sure you don't mean to apologize for that – utterly damnable though it is – (& perhaps the insult wasn't in a letter after all). Anyhow, I wish I could see you on Tuesday, but we don't get back till about 7.30, which is too late, I'm afraid.

Perhaps you'll be passing through again – if not, you &
Jacques must come down here. I don't believe you've ever
seen this place, anyhow not since it was lived in & had
something like a garden – 20 daffodils & ½ a dozen cro-
cuses. It's far the loveliest place in the world.

Yrs V.W.

We must have been just before you at Harbour View.

France 1922

Virginia was 40. In the previous 10 years, she had published The Voyage Out, Night and Day *and* Monday or Tuesday. *She had married Leonard Woolf in 1912 and they leased Hogarth House in Richmond in 1915 and, in 1919, bought Monks House, near Lewes as a country retreat where they could write. She started the* Hogarth Press *with Leonard in 1917. Jacques's letter to which Virginia is responding is lost.*

In 1922, Gwen and Jacques were both 37 and had begun to establish themselves as artists, as had their friends Eric Gill and Stanley Spencer. They moved to Villa Adèle near the town of Vence in Provence in October 1920 with their two daughters, Elisabeth, born on Boxing Day 1916, and Sophie, born 20th December 1919. Jacques's 'disseminated sclerosis' was making him weaker, unable to paint for weeks at a time.

Monks House, Rodmell,
Lewes   Aug. 25th [1922]

Dear Jacques,

Anyhow you haven't forgotten one feature in your old friend's character – vanity. I enjoyed your praises [*of* Monday or Tuesday *published in 1921*] immensely, & Gwen's, & felt quite set up for many days. I rather expect abuse for that book. Now you must give me your opinion of my novel [Jacob's Room] which comes out soon – foreigner you may be, but you're a highly interesting character still.

Shall we really come out sometime next January? Could you find us rooms in your village? We talk perpetually of

going abroad, but I want to settle in where one can read &
write, & if you were there it would be great fun. Then
perhaps we could talk of some of our arrears. I feel a little
shy, do you? Not fundamentally, superficially. My impression is that we used to argue a great deal about the way to
live. Now we have solved all that. You have a house in France,
& we in Richmond. It's rather nice, shabby, ancient, very
solid, & incredibly untidy (I'm talking of Hogarth House)
but then we print all over the place. One of Ka's gallant
youths – I mean the sort of person Ka used to have about
– is our partner [*Ralph Partridge*]. We meet at lunch & tea.
We gossip. The poor young man tries to tell us what Lytton
Strachey thinks about Proust (he lives with Lytton & has
married Carrington). Then I go up to London: walk the
streets, on the excuse of buying something – nothing so
amazing; drop in to tea at the 1917 Club, where one
generally falls into gloom at the extreme insignificance
– dowdiness of the intellectual race – darkies, actresses,
cranks, Alix, James – that's the sort of creature one meets
there. Well, I don't boast. I'm only one of them myself,
but inwardly one still feels young & arrogant & frightfully
sharp set. I can't resist boasting still – can you? & trying to
talk people down. Still, we have grown a little mellow. Eve-
ryone in Gordon Square is now famous.

Clive has taken to high society. I assure you, he's a raging
success, & his bon mots are quoted by lovely but incredibly
silly ladies. Really they give parties to meet Clive Bell.
Maynard of course scarcely belongs to private life any
more, save that he has fallen in love with Lydia Lopokhova,

which is, to me, endearing. Nessa & Duncan potter along in extreme obscurity. That is all I can think of at the moment, & I am afraid that it may sound vague & dismal in your ears. The truth is you must write me a proper letter, & expose yourself as I hereby expose myself.

I feel that in the great age of the world, before this present puling generation had come along, you & I & that remarkable figure Gwen Darwin, were all congenial spirits. By the way you'll have to give up calling Woolf, Woolf: Leonard, that is his name. I assure you, I couldn't have married anyone else – But when Ka praises Will the sound is unpleasant in my ears. So I refrain. I have nothing whatever to say against Ka & Will. At first sight he is a mere sandhopper; but later I think he has some sort of spine – indeed, he's a muscular little man, considering his size. Ka, of course, keeps a medicine chest & doses the village, & gets into a blue dress trimmed with fur for tea, when county motor cars arrive, & she is much in her element. Is this malicious? Slightly, perhaps, but you will understand.

I wish I could discuss the art of writing with you at the present moment. I am ashamed, or perhaps proud to say how much of my time is spent in thinking, thinking, thinking, about literature. It is a dangerous seed to plant in your children. Still, I doubt whether any thing else in life is much worth having – so there is the philosophy of an old woman of 40. Do you maintain that one can think about painting? Is Gwen Raverat still so extreme? And what about Lady Darwin [*Maud, Gwen's mother*] & dear poor pincushion Eily?

But I am drivelling. Tell me when you write if there are

any good French books; and say if you would like me to send you anything from England –

Love to Gwen,
Yours ever
Virginia Woolf

Gwen Raverat, self portrait, pencil

It can be conjectured that Virginia sent Jacques one of the first copies of Jacob's Room, *since it was published on 26th October 1922 and here he is finishing it in early December.*

dictated to Gwen Raverat
Villa Adèle, Vence, A.M.   December 1922

Dear Virginia,

This is principally to say that we hope you have not forgotten or given up your plan of visiting Vence sometime in the winter, or the spring, or even in the summer or autumn, when it's loveliest of all. And also to say that I've just finished *Jacob's Room*. I like it far better than your 2 earlier novels, though perhaps not quite so much as some of the things in *Monday or Tuesday*. But I have 2 serious criticisms to make: 1) Your suggestion that a toad is really only an insect after all, and 2) your feminine spelling of the Boulevard Raspail, which seems to me quite inexcusable even if you do think women are always nicer than men (almost the opposite of my own experience). In spite of these blemishes I liked it very much, & we'll talk of it more in detail when you come. Did you ever get my last letter? I still think your prose is VERY GOOD INDEED.

Yrs ever
Jacques Raverat

(Jacques is getting very fat, which annoys him very much indeed. Gwen)

Jacob's Room *had sold 850 copies by December 3rd.*

Hogarth House,
Paradise Road,
Richmond,
Surrey   Dec. 10 1922

My dear Jacques,

It was very nice to get your letter – to which Gwen's handwriting adds an unmistakable smack of that lost but
unforgotten woman. I'm glad you liked *Jacob* better than
the other novels; one always wishes the last to be best. I'm
not blind, though, to its imperfections – indeed it's more
an experiment than an achievement. Is your art as chaotic
as ours? I feel that for us writers the only chance now is to
go out into the desert & peer about, like devoted scapegoats, for some sign of a path. I expect you got through
your discoveries sometime earlier. All this, however, we will
chatter about endlessly when we meet.

But when? I say the end of March. This depends, for us,
upon arrangements with the *Nation*, for which Leonard
has to write a weekly article on foreign politics. Still, we do
mean to come, & have promised to take a boat from Marseilles & go on to Spain to stay with a solitary eccentric
young man, called Brenan, who is trying to learn to write
upon a mountain near Granada. Do you know him?

Ought we to arrange about rooms? Perhaps Gwen would
tell me sometime closer to March. I heard praises of your

HOGARTH HOUSE
PARADISE ROAD
RICHMOND
SURREY

Telephone : Richmond 496

Dec. 10th 1922

My dear Jacques,

It was very nice to get your letter – to which Gwen's
handwriting adds an unmistakable smack of that
lost but unforgotten woman.   I'm glad you liked
Jacob better than the other novels; one always wishes the
last to be best. I'm not blind, though, to its imperfections –
indeed this more an experiment than an achievement.
Is your art as chaotic as ours?   I feel that for us
writers the only chance now is to go out into the
desert & peer about, like devoted scapegoats, for some
sign of a path.   I expect you got through your
discoveries sometimes earlier. All this, however, we will
chatter about endlessly when we meet.
                But when?   I say the end of March.
This depends, for us, upon arrangements with the Nation,
for which Leonard has to write a weekly article on
foreign politics. Still, we do mean to come, &
have promised to take a boat from Marseilles
& go on to Spain to stay with a solitary eccentric
young man, called Brenan, who is trying
to learn to write upon a mountain near Granada.
Do you know him?
                            Ought we to arrange about

pictures from Roger Fry the other night. He thinks you are now doing the interesting things – but I don't know if his praises, or anyone's praises, mean much to you. We are so lonely & separated in our adventures as writers & painters. I never dare praise pictures, though I have my own opinions. Raspail was spelt wrong owing to Duncan & Vanessa, whom I consulted. A letter more or less means nothing to them. Toads are (essentially) insects, I maintain. Women may be worse, or may be better, than men; but surely the opinions of the writer of *Jacob's Room* on that point, or any other, are not *my* opinions. This is a very old quarrel though.

I'm glad you are fat; for then you are warm & mellow & generous & creative. I find that unless I weigh 9½ stones I hear voices & see visions & can neither write nor sleep. This is a necessity, I suppose, to part with youth & beauty, but I think there are compensations –

Please write again, if it doesn't bore you. I enjoyed your letter so much, & imagine your whole existence, no doubt a little wrong, as I walk with my dog, in Richmond Park.

The Hogarth Press is branching out in January with 2 partners [*Dadie Rylands and Marjorie Thompson, later to marry the philosopher C.E.M. Joad*]. Haven't you some writing up your sleeve?

Yours ever
Virginia Woolf

Jeu de Boules, Vence, by Gwen Raverat, wood engraving
(reduced in size), 1922

France 1923

On the 27th March, the Woolfs travelled via Paris to Madrid, and then on to Granada and Yegen where they stayed with Gerald Brenan (the 'Englishman's Castle').

Hotel Inglés,
Madrid   Good Friday [March 30th 1923]

My dear Jacques,

    Domestic uncertainties have prevented me from writing to you – that is to say, the *Nation*, the newspaper for which Leonard wrote, has been bought by Maynard Keynes, & Leonard just lost his job, which ruined us, & has now been made Literary Editor, which is almost as bad. It means that we must be back punctually on April 27th & thus shan't get to Vence. This is a great disappointment; but next year? It will have to be arranged somehow. Will Gwen be over again? Don't let her choose August if she is. Meanwhile, I hope you will occasionally send a letter. Only friendship dictates this. Never was there such a pen, and as for Hotels, the spirits of the damned inhabit them. It is a superb country all the same, as we came through yesterday. Still, I was impressed by the South of France – not by the midlands. I felt a kind of levity & frivolity & congeniality upon me with the first sight of Dieppe. How much more enjoyable in some queer way France is than England! But how does one learn the language? I must & will. I want to know how the French think. After the English, they seem so natural, so much akin to all one likes.

Here we have been following the Crucifixion & the Last Supper through the streets, & again I felt entirely sympathetic, which one couldn't imagine doing in Piccadilly say, or the Earls Court Road [*In October 1911*] – where you and Gwen once lived, if I remember, before you made your grand attack upon Bloomsbury, & left us. Is this right? You see I am still reconstructing your past, from fragments, mostly false, I daresay. You were a man of convictions, in which you were confirmed by marrying a Darwin, of all races the most monolithic. I was in Cambridge last month, & there started up, in the Shove's drawing room, a military man, of upright bearing & manly spirit, whom I thought to be a friend of Gerald's youth, quite out of place in literary society – but it was Mr Cornford! [*Francis Cornford had married Gwen's cousin Frances Darwin, the poet. Gerald Shove was an Apostle and Fellow of Kings College who married Fredegund Maitland.*] Good Heavens! Last time he was wearing a French peasants' blouse & a red tie. There is a great deal of mystic religion about. I wish one had the cruelty of youth. I've been asked to advise a woman as to the souls of the dead – can they come back? As I'm never quite sure which is which – spirit, matter, truth, falsehood & so on – I can't speak out as roundly as a Darwin should. Or is Gwen not an agnostic?

Are you painting? Will they be shown in London? Are they good? And in what direction are they tending? I wanted to buy a seascape by Matisse the other day, but the price was tremendous.

But this is trivial gossip, & we must go out & dine. I find

you easy to write to, however – which I mean as a very great compliment. (You remember how vain I always was).

Now we go on for 10 days to the Englishman's Castle near Granada, & then home to Maynard, to politics, to printing, to whatever life may be said to be. I've no room to go into the matter further, alas.

Love to Gwen.

Yours ever,

V.W.

The Raverat's great friends from Cambridge, Hugh and Jessie Stewart and their daughters, rented the villa next door all that winter and spring bringing welcome distraction from Jacques's illness, the effects of which were becoming more severe. Hugh had christened Elisabeth Raverat in Cambridge in 1917.

dictated to Gwen Raverat
Villa Adèle,
Vence, A.M.   4th May 1923

My dear Virginia.

It was very disappointing. I cannot help thinking that you chose wrong. We didn't actually have any snow here, as you did at Granada (I read that in a paper.) Certainly then next year; but must we really wait till then? I seem to remember that you don't mind the heat; didn't you go to Spain once in the middle of the summer? And I'm sure it isn't as hot here & it's really so much the loveliest time. Anyhow do think of it & let us make a definite plan, as soon as it's possible for you. I'm glad you like France. I think one enjoys life there more than in England somehow. Besides – O what I really mean is, that Frenchmen are so much nicer, better, & wiser, more intelligent, than Englishmen; & they like me better too. But on the other hand I still have that absurd preference for English women, which has ruined my life. That sort of attraction is an odd thing isn't it. It doesn't seem to depend in any direct way on beauty, or on any of the qualities I really like or admire in mind or character. I suppose it's a mystery or something of that sort. Now you are not to take these remarks as a basis for reconstructing my history; you really haven't sufficient data you know. But I must admit I am extremely curious how you do reconstruct it. Fragments can be so misleading. For instance what you call – quite wrongly – our grand attack on Bloomsbury. I assure you there was never anything of the sort. It was rather a flight from it all – because I suddenly felt as if I couldn't breathe in that air a minute longer. It would be easier to explain in conversation than in a letter. Did I really have convictions 10 years ago? If I did I must have caught them in the English air & from my English friends; for I'm sure they were not natural to me; & I assure you there's very little left of them now, in spite of having married a Darwin – (or perhaps because). (But seriously I suppose Rupert had more to do with it than anyone, in those days.)

Yes isn't it horrible about all that mystic religion. You should hear Gwen about it; she is nothing so perplexed as an agnostic, but a militant atheist.

You ask if I am painting. Yes, as well as I can with my left hand now; & there are 6 or 8 things of mine at Turner's – rather old ones, – 2 or 3 years ago. I dare say he'd shew them to you if you ask; and are they good? Well, it's very difficult to know, till one's dead. When I think of Rembrandt & Renoir I feel rather small & humbled but then when I see the works of almost any of my contemporaries I feel quite cheered up again & think that mine isn't so bad after all. Anyhow I suppose it doesn't matter much; it helps to pass the time as people say. As for my direction the Lord only knows. Southeast I should think, more or less. And one paints the pictures one can & not the pictures one wants to paint. I should like to paint calm happy pictures of people with lovely bodies & no minds at all. Matisse is great fun; but he's rather like champagne & sweet champagne at that. I don't believe he'll keep & I'm sure I shouldn't like to have him every day for breakfast, dinner, lunch & tea. I suppose he & Bonnard & Valloton are the best of the men over 50. Of those under, Segonzac & Marchand. Segonzac is the more exciting, but I think Marchand will go further & last longer.

Tell me what you think about writers, & tell me also what you are writing now. But I babble on endlessly. I could go on writing to you like this for hours; so I might as well stop now. But it will be fun seeing you, & talking again & comparing our experiences of life. Oh do tell me, what books you read most & oftenest. I find Pepys & *Les Mille et Une Nuits* (Madrus) are the ones I never get tired of. Gwen has got writer's cramp, so I shall *have* to stop. Do write again. Gwen sends her love – if you will accept it from so extreme a person.

Yrs Jacques Raverat

Note: Why do the French like thick muddy purple ink like this?

As editor of the Athenaeum, *John Middleton Murry promoted and employed his wife and, after her death, 'boiled her bones', as Virginia put it, in his magazine, the* Adelphi.

Hogarth House,
Richmond   July 30th 1923

My dear Jacques,

   I only got your letter two hours ago, on my English breakfast tray, with its bacon & egg: & I will answer at once. No, no, no. Nothing you said offended me; all delighted me; & I should have written ages ago if I had not always said 'I'll write Jacques a nice long letter' – & so waited for the proper moment, & wrote meanwhile myriads of dreary drudgery. I find I never write to people I like. Jacques & Gwen require a good state of mind: whereas, – now you shall fill in the names of our old friends who can be put off with miserable relics.

   We are all packed to go to Sussex tomorrow. This conveys nothing to you who have never seen the *Hogarth Press*. We travel with a selection of our books packed in hampers. Add to this a dog & a tortoise, bought for 2/- yesterday in the High Street. My husband presides with considerable mastery – poor devil, I make him pay for his unfortunate mistake in being born a Jew by discharging the whole business of life. This induces in me a sense of the trans-itoriness of existence, & the unreality of matter, which is highly con-genial & comfortable. Now what do *you* think real? Gwen used to have views about that. Gwen was a highly dogmatic woman. Her breed is, alas, quite extinct. I assure you, I can knock over the freest thinker & boldest liver with the brush of a feather – nincompoop though I am, as far as logic goes.

This brings me, rather helter skelter, (but forgive thimble headedness in your old friend) – to the question of the religious revival; which concerns you both a good deal more nearly than you suspect. On my way back from Spain I stayed a week in Paris & there met Hope Mirrlees & Jane Harrison. [*Jane Harrison was Newnham College, Cambridge's first ever research fellow in 1898 when Gwen met her. She later decamped to Paris with Hope Mirrlees.*] This gallant old lady, very white, hoary, & sublime in a lace mantilla, took my fancy greatly; partly for her superb high thinking agnostic ways, partly for her appearance. 'Alas,' she said, 'you & your sister & perhaps Lytton Strachey are the only ones of the younger generation I can respect. You alone carry on the traditions of our day.' This referred to the miserable defection of Fredegund (mass; confession; absolution, & the rest of it.) [*Fredegund Shove converted to Catholicism in 1927.*] 'There are thousands of Darwins,' I said, to cheer her up. 'Thousands of Darwins!' she shrieked, clasping her mittened hands, & raising her eyes to Heaven. 'The Darwins are the blackest traitors of them all! With that name!' she cried. 'That inheritance! That magnificent record in the past!' 'Surely,' I cried, 'Our Gwen is secure?' 'Our Gwen,' she replied, 'goes to Church, (if not mass, still church) every Sunday of her life. Her marriage, of course, may have weakened her brain. Jacques is, unfortunately, French. A wave of Catholicism has invaded the

young Frenchmen. Their children are baptized; their –'. Here I stopped her. 'Good God,' I said, 'I will never speak to them again! What's more, I've just written a flippant, frivolous, atheistic letter to that very household, which will arrive precisely as the Host is elevated; they'll spit me from their lips, spurn me from their hearts – &, in short, religion has accomplished one more of her miracles, & destroyed a friendship which I'm sure began in our mothers' wombs!' All this eloquence left me dejected as a shovelful of cinders. Next week arrived your letter, which was the greatest relief in the world. Gwen is a militant atheist: the world renews itself: there is solid ground beneath my feet. I at once sent word to dear old Jane, who replied, a little inconsistently, 'Thank God'.

But speaking seriously, (& I need not say that the hand of art has slightly embellished the preceding) this religious revival is a glum business. Poor Middleton Murry has had a conversion, which has had an odious Bantam – the *Adelphi* – which I wish you'd take in & comment upon monthly. I'm too much prejudiced to be fair to him. As literature, it seems to me worthless – (only strong words are out of place:) it seems to me mediocre then. The spirit that inspires it, with its unction, & hypocrisy, & God is love, which still leaves room for flea bites: pin pricks, & advertising astuteness, would enrage, were it not that there's something so mild & wobbly about that too that I can't waste good wrath. Most of my friends find it deplorable. Ka, the usual exception, rather likes it. But the story of the Murrys is long & elaborate, & I'm getting so harassed by household affairs that perhaps I'd better stop.

(Leonard: Here's a man from the typewriter shop. Shall we be rash and buy a new one?

Cook: I think I'd better make the pie tomorrow. Monday meat is never trustworthy.

Virginia: I shall have to take my pink dress, if we're going to stay with Maynard.

Leonard: Well you can't take your pink dress, because the luggage has gone.

Virginia: Gone? Good God! Gone?

Leonard: I told you twenty times it was going at eleven. etc. etc.)

I knew both the Murrys. Please read Katherine [Mansfield]'s works, & tell me your opinion. My theory is that while she possessed the most amazing *senses* of her generation so that she could actually reproduce this room for instance, with its fly, clock, dog, tortoise to the life, she was as weak as water: as insipid, & a great deal more commonplace, when she had to use her mind. That is, she can't put thoughts, or feelings, or subtleties of any kind into her characters, without at once becoming, where she's serious, hard, &, where she's sympathetic, sentimental. Her first story which we printed, *Prelude*, was pure observation & therefore exquisite. I could not read her latest ['The Canary']. But prejudice may be at work here too. As for the Sitwells, though I paid 3/6 to hear Edith vociferate her poems, accompanied by a small & nimble orchestra, through a megaphone, I understood so little that I could not Judge. I know Osbert slightly. They take themselves very seriously.

They descend from George IVth. They look like Regency bucks. They have a mother who was in prison. They probably need careful reading, which I have never given them, & thus incline to think them vigorous, but unimportant, acrobats. Literature is in a queer way; however; as I shall explain next letter. By the way, do send me your version of Mrs Litchfield's remarks, on my article. [*Henrietta Litchfield ('Aunt Etty') was Gwen's supporter in the Darwin clan. The article was 'To Spain', published in the* Nation.] Gerald Brenan's aunt sent him the same unfortunate work, picked out with red lines in ink. She was outraged. (She is 85) She said it was done for notoriety & was only printed because 'Mrs. Woolf has the dibbs, & would cut Mr Woolf short if he didn't.' But Mrs L., being Gwen's Aunt, is much too refined to say that.

What a letter! What a letter! It is like the interminable monologue of an old village woman standing at her door. Each time you say good day & try to move off, she bethinks her of something fresh & it all begins again. And my hand shakes, so that I can't write legibly. I have a queer illness, which consists of a permanent slight fever, which the Dr. diagnosed consumption, but have almost cured now by injecting pneumonia germs in multitudes. This must be my excuse for febrile verbosity. Please write to Monks House, Rodmell, Lewes.

Ever yours

V.W.

Jacques Raverat, by Gwen Raverat, oils, c. 1924

Gwen's first cousin Frances had married the poet Francis Cornford, a protégé of Jane Harrison's. Some believe Frances's famous poem, 'O fat white woman whom nobody loves, / Why do you walk through the fields in gloves' was written about Gwen when Jacques was dallying as to whether he loved Ka Cox or her. Depression led Frances to retreat from the world for large parts of her life.

dictated to Gwen Raverat
Villa Adèle,
Vence, A.M.   14th September 1923

My dear Virginia,

What a splendid letter that was & how we laughed over your conversation with Jane – Gwen of course was very indignant & muttered things about a libel action; & indeed I think Jane is a wicked old woman to go about spreading malicious rumours like that. It's enough to ruin anyone's character & reputation. And when one thinks what an incorrigible old mystic she is herself. Of course it is true that Gwen had her children christened but if she (Jane) knew in what spirit it was done – i.e. as a kind of spiritual vaccination – I don't think she *could* accuse Gwen of Christianity.

No, Darwins are Darwins still, all except Frances. We try & keep that as dark as we can & it all goes to shew the dangers of psycho analysis. But as for myself my case, as you would imagine, is not so simple. Ever since the age of

My dear Virginia. What a splendid letter that was &
how we laughed over your conversation with Jane.
Gwen of course was very indignant & muttered things
about a libel action; & indeed I think Jane is a
wicked old woman to go about spreading malicious
rumours like that. It's enough to ruin anyone's character
& reputation.   And when one thinks what an
incorrigible old mystic she is herself. Of course
if it is true that Gwen had her children christened
but if she ~~knew~~ (Jane) knew in what spirit it was
done — ie as a kind of spiritual vaccination —
I don't think she could accuse Gwen of Christianity.
No, Darwins are Darwins still, all except
Frances. We try & keep that as dark as we can
& it all goes to shew the dangers of ~~psyc~~ psycho analysis.
But as for myself, my case, as you would imagine,
is not so simple. Ever since the age of 25 or thereabouts, perhaps it was when I married, my
interest in the Eternal Problems & the
Ultimate Truth had been steadily declining,
until some years ago it went out altogether
I suppose I should have to submit to being called an
agnostic, but not by my friends; & not only in the

Did you know Jacques
has a beard now,
a Red beard? GR

Did you know Jacques has a beard now, a *red beard?* GR

25 or thereabouts, perhaps it was when I married, my interest in the Eternal Problems & the Ultimate Truth had been steadily declining, until some years ago it went out altogether. I suppose I should have to submit to being called an agnostic, but not by friends; & not only in the sense of not knowing, but not wanting to know – I wouldn't give half a crown for the riddle of the universe, or for any answer to it, & what's more I don't believe there is one. I never think about these things; (they are an Awful Bore) except par esprit de contradiction. I mean that if the religious (I don't often meet them) seem to me almost incredibly childish & silly; conversely a dogmatic atheist like one or two we know, always make me feel that there must be something in Christianity after all. Don't *you* think that people's opinions about things are not really very important or very interesting? They are always much too simple and how absurd they all seem to the next generation.

What matters is their reactions, sensations, actions, passions, & pleasures. That's the sort of things that seem real to me if you ask. And then immediate, particular & concrete things, like boots & trees & mackerel. I am sure that neither practical life nor general ideas have any reality at all; but on the contrary, painting, food & drink ... love making in the most literal sense ... music; hills & towns – & Oh – sleep. I feel that I am writing with a naïveté which ill becomes my age. But it doesn't matter. I'm even old enough not to mind being thought foolish. One gets to realise that there are not many people wiser than oneself. I think that's one of the awful tragedies of life. Anyhow enough of all this nonsense.

I agree with a good deal that you say about Katherine Mansfield, but I don't admire her even as much as you do. It seems to me all too mechanical & too photographic to talk of senses; & so much of it was just rather a cheap trick; but I think I never read her first story *Prelude*, which you talk of; I can't really remember. But I read the other day a book which rather impressed me: it is the *Poor Man* by Stella Benson. Do you know it, or her? It was I thought a little unbalanced in the composition, but its rather remarkable to combine such wit with a power for laying bare all the things one is so dreadfully ashamed of in human nature & human life. It really makes one writhe sometimes. I read enormous quantities of what I suppose one must call bad books; partly because they are much less effort to read than good books; & then I read all the good books when I was young. And there are so many hours every day that I have to waste while my supply of nervous energy is winding up again for 2 or 3 hours real work. Well, I wonder if you ever read bad books, I find it an extremely interesting study & very illuminating about human nature, though not usually in the way intended by the authors. And sometimes they are so very nearly good. The ideas often are. Yes *do* explain in your next letter, as you promised, what is the matter with literature; it certainly is in a queer state. I want to know what you're working at, if it's not a secret; are you writing another novel, or what? Do try & let us know as soon as you can more or less when you plan

Jacques Raverat, by Gwen Raverat, pencil, 1912?

to come out & see us, so that we can keep the time clear for you. And do really come. And in the meanwhile write.

Yrs Jacques Raverat.

I do hope that you're now quite cured & quite well again. Being ill is I sometimes think almost intolerable, but I rather despise the people who aren't – don't you? I'm sure we have a finer sensitiveness & keener appreciation of life. How is Maynard getting on with his Russian lady? I shall probably hear a lot about it from Margaret but I somehow imagine your version will be different.

By 1923 Virginia was becoming widely known as a novelist and critic and was enjoying being at the hub of a social scene in London. Not only was Ka Cox important to both the Raverats and Virginia, but Virginia was to find her intimate friendship important a few years later.

Hogarth House,
Paradise Road,
Richmond   Nov. 4th 1923

My dear Jacques,

You were saying that you would like a little gossip about Maynard & Lydia. On Sept. 7th we went to stay with them at Studland – a ducal house [*The Knoll, the Dorset seaside retreat of the Duke of Hamilton*], in which they fared, rather uneasily I thought, because the duke's servants were in the pantry; and Lydia's habits, of course, are not ducal. I do not know how far I transgress the bounds of good taste, if I allude (oh it must be in a whisper, only in the presence of Gwen) to – well they're called Sanitary Towels – you see blue bundles discreetly hidden beneath lace in the windows of small drapers. When used they should be burnt. Lydia, whose father was porter in a Petersburg hotel, and whose entire life has been spent hopping from foot to foot with the daughters of publicans, did not know this perhaps: the most binding of all laws of female life. (Ask any Darwin, excepting Mrs Litchfield – they'll tell you). She put her week's supply on the grate. The grate was filled with white shavings. Imagine the consequences. There she left them. The cooks husband, & Duke's valet, did the room. Soon the Cook herself requested to speak with the lady. Never was such a scene, it is said, as shook the rafters, – rage, tears, despair, outrage, horror, retribution, reconciliation; & – if you know Lydia you'll see how naturally it follows – lifelong friendship upon a basis of – well, bloody rags. Really, there is a curious feeling about that menage, as well may be with such a foundation. Lydia has the soul of a squirrel: anything nicer you can't conceive; she sits by the hour polishing the sides of her nose with her front paws. But, poor little wretch, trapped in Bloomsbury, what can she do but learn Shakespeare by heart? I assure you it's tragic to see her sitting down to King Lear. Nobody can take her seriously: every nice young man kisses her. Then she flies into a rage & says she is like Vanessa, like Virginia, like Alix Sargent Florence, or Ka Cox – a seerious wooman.

Ka Cox dined with us two nights ago. Is malice allowed? Is it deducted from the good marks I have acquired, or hope to acquire with the Raverat family? But then you've known the worst of me – my incorrigible mendacity; my leering, sneering, undependable disposition. You take me as I am, & make allowances for the sake of old days. Well, then, Ka is *intolerably dull*. I am quoting my husband: I am not quite of that opinion myself: but why, I ask, condescend to the Woolfs? Why be so damned matronly? Why always talk about Will – that parched & pinched little hob goblin, whom I like very much but think an incorrigibly bad painter, as if he were Shelley, Mr Gladstone, Byron & Helen of Troy in one? I don't carry on about Leonard like that, nor yet Gwen about Jacques. What I suspect is that dear old Ka feels the waves of life withdraw, & there, perched high on her rock [*her house in Cornwall*], makes these frantic efforts to pretend, to make the Woolfs believe, that she is still visited by the waters of the great sea.

Indeed, once upon a time, when we all swooned upon her in our love affairs & collapsed in our nervous breakdowns, she was. She was wetted punctually & shone in her passive way, like some faintly coloured sea anemone, who never budges, never stings, never – but I am getting wrapped up in words.

Anyhow, both Leonard and I lost our tempers. We said nothing. We went to bed in the devil of a gloom. Are we like that? we said. Are we middle aged & content? Do we look like old cabbages? Is life entirely a matter of retrospect & county families & trying to impress people with ringing up men at the foreign office about French conscription of Natives in Africa? No, no, no. Let us change the subject.

Duncan has just been in to tea. I may tell you it is rather a fine November day, but dark about half past four. Duncan was going on to Twickenham to see his mother to choose some silks for a chair cover – bright sunlight being essential. It's no good. She goes to the window & shows him the church all lit up. Off he wanders murmuring something about getting there by day break – Half his buttons seemed to be off; his braces are too long. He has always to be hitching himself together; & odd bits of shirt stick out. Anrep has done a mosaic which is said to be very good

78

[*Boris Anrep's mosaic pavement for 'The Blake Room' at the Tate*]; Segonzac has been admiring the London group; Sickert has surpassed himself [*Walter Sickert's* The Bar-Parlour *purchased by Maynard Keynes*]; Alix & James Strachey think we should go to war with France. Lytton is buying a house at Hungerford [*Ham Spray*].

What other news is there? Very little I think of interest, so far as facts go. And to convey feelings is too difficult. I try, but I invariably make enemies. I go to parties, very occasionally, & there get rather random headed, & *say too much*. I assure you it's fatal – but I never can resist the desire for intimacy, or reconcile myself to the fact that all human relations are bound to be unsatisfactory. Are they? I rather expect Jacques, in his thick black beard, surveying the country from his motor car, knows all about it. I still play my game of making up Jacques & Gwen as I walk about London. No doubt I shall be picked off by a motor omnibus in the thick of it. After half an hour's acute discomfort, should we settle down to the old relationship, whatever it was? Jacques I think was rather dictatorial; he called us silly women; he said the Oliviers were *real* [*Margery, Brynhild, Daphne and Noel, the four beautiful Neo-Pagan daughters of Sir Sydney Olivier*]: but not most people. Gwen sat on the floor & said something very positive – being, poor woman, a Darwin to the back bone; & Virginia, of course, shied & shilly-shallied, & – no, you must write Virginia's part, because she is, oddly enough, the last woman I have any idea of.

About coming to Vence – this must be done somehow, & I aim at Easter, or later, or earlier. But we are tied by the navel string to the *Nation*; & – what awful, indecent things I keep thinking of this evening!

Please write someday soon; & explain what you think about, as you survey the world. And please think kindly of me. How I depend upon my friends! You wouldn't believe it, either of you.

Ever yours
V.W.

Babette Giroux (the Raverat's nanny),
by Gwen Raverat, pencil, c. 1923.

Monastry from the Ramparts, Vence, by Jacques Raverat, oils, 1923

Antibes, by Jacques Raverat, oils, 1923

Tall Houses at Vence, by Jacques Raverat, oils, 1923

Baous from Place St Michel, Vence, by Jacques Raverat, oils, 1922

France 1924

Vence, La Place en Été, by Gwen Raverat, wood engraving
(reduced in size), 1923

*The Woolfs moved to Tavistock Square, Bloomsbury, from Hog-
arth House, Richmond the month this letter was written. Adrian,
Virginia's brother, and his wife, Karin Stephen, were training to
be psychoanalysts. His analyis put a strain on their marriage caus-
ing a temporary separation.*

52 Tavistock Square,
London, WC1   March 8th 1924

My dear Jacques,

   This you see [*her new address*] is the reason why I haven't
written & can't write now & won't be able, so far as I can
see to cross the channel this year – a new house, to which
we move in a few days, which has had to be cleaned,
scoured, painted & lighted, all in a hurry, leaving me a mere
drudge, without a thought in my head, or, what's much
worse, a penny in my purse. I don't therefore see how we
can possibly take precedence of your better off friend. Let
us creep into a cranny, if we can come. Otherwise assume
we can't.

   But that's no reason why our letters should languish. You
don't want to hear about my new house, I know by experience. It has a basement for the press, & a large studio: 2
floors full of solicitors; L & I on top looking at all the
glories of London, which are romantically, sentimentally,
incredibly dear to me. The Imperial Hotel, all pink & blue,
in Russell Square: St Pancras Church spire, carved from
white plaster – do you know it? These are the things I love,

The Balcony (Villa Adèle), by Gwen Raverat,
wood engraving (actual size), 1926

better than olive trees & mountains, but not so much as Jacques & Gwen, after all.

You said very tactfully in your last letter, Why did Adrian & Karin separate, or rather how did he stand that d----d American all these years? I must say your language is a trifle strong. She is a good, honest woman; & in her place I'd have done the same, & in his too. Incompatible, is what they say; & this they've realised for 8 years, & ground their teeth over, while appearing in public the most love-locked of couples. We Stephens are difficult, especially as the race tapers out, towards its finish – such cold fingers, so fastidious. so critical, such tastes. My madness has saved me; but Adrian is sane – that's all the light I can throw.

I dare not go on, because my brain is in splinters, & my handwriting like drifts of wreckage. Do you remember [*Saxon*] Sydney-Turner [*a friend of Thoby Stephen*]? a phantom, gliding like a moon beam through my Thursday evenings, & settling still on one chair for 6 hours on end? He's coming here with his old mother. I forget whom you like, & whom dislike. Don't you think you might write me your memories of all our friends? There are the Oliviers now, whom I meet about, with their beautiful glass eyes, glazed & fixed & melancholy – Noel always enraptures me. She cries over Rupert's letters, she tells me; & really, I fall in love with her, being so sentimental, for doing it. Bryn has been divorced – that you know. Poor Hugh, so I'm told, spent his Sundays making wooden beds, for Sherrard to step into on Monday when he'd gone: he was always making things – Ka is watching the spring, & Will [*Arnold-Forster, whom Ka had married*] has written a little book which we are printing. Now, why don't you & Gwen write us a pamphlet about art? or life? *This is serious.* Something profound yet sparkling.

I'll write again: so do you.

Ever yours

V.W.

Eily's visit to Vence just before this letter was written was very helpful to Gwen. Gide's visit that spring was more uneasy. He had kept in touch with Jacques through Paul Valéry whom Jacques came to prefer of the two. Other visitors that spring included Jean Marchand, the painter, and Ethne Pryor, whose son Mark was to marry my mother Sophie Raverat in September 1940.

dictated to Gwen Raverat
Vence,
Villa Adèle   13th May 1924

My dear Virginia,

One ought to answer letters, except in anger, at once. By the time they've lain weeks in a drawer, one's forgotten – of the brilliant & witty repartees, which the first reading brought to mind. But then I suppose we should spend our lives letter-writing, & I don't know that I'm quite prepared for that, though there is a good deal to be said for it; specially writing letters to people like you. Or rather receiving them I mean. One can say so neatly things which would be carried away in the flood of conversation, & then there isn't that absurd shyness creeping in which you always talk about. Anyhow do remember that your letters are always a very great pleasure to me, & write again soon.

Of course what I really need is a Boswell; if Gwen had any sense of her duties as a wife, had any conscience of her duties to posterity, she might undertake to note down some of my most pregnant epigrams. When Frances was here last, she went as far as to buy a little note book for this purpose, quite seriously, & that shewed the right spirit; but she could only remember one quite prehistoric, though still quite true, remark: That woman's place is the bed. And the note book since has lain empty & dusty. Of course I am immensely flattered that you should seriously propose to print a book for me (I am truly) but there are several difficulties & objections. I don't know about Gwen, I should think she will probably send you some immense manuscript one of these days, as she hasn't got quite enough to do with nursing me & looking after her children & painting 10 hours a day & doing woodcuts at intervals; but for myself, in the first place, I can't write in English & you wouldn't print things in French of course. I hope you will be polite enough to say that I obviously can; I shall not be deceived. In the second place the very thought of writing makes me feel quite sick; (except letters to you.) I might *have* to do it, if I became blind, but nothing short of that would drive me to it.

However I was thinking over some of the things that I might try to write. You mention the memories of our friends, or sometime friends. But they would nearly all be completely unprintable for the next 50 years at least, if one told the truth. (And by the way I want to talk to you sometime about that matter of truth in literature. Why are all you writers such bloody liars?) Then of course one might write one's own confessions; that I should think would have to wait 500 years, till my bones could no longer blush. And I don't think I could write either brightly or profoundly on either life or art; I know nothing about them. But I thought of a little series of Sex Primers. What Young Men ought *Really* to know. Self Abuse for Self Made Men. Etc. etc. But dear me how coarse I am getting. These might be a sound commercial proposition, whilst presented in a tasteful literary form; & appeal to all classes & all ages. But enough of this trifling. Have you read Ulysses? I drifted laboriously through it in the winter. I thought it the dreariest book I had ever read. There is a name for that sort of thing. It is Onanism. And it ought to be a warning to the young.

Then the 2 posthumous volumes of Proust, which were after all a little disappointing. It's all so like a man trying to remember a tune on the piano, & going round & round in circles. The whole of Gibbon for the first time in my life. And Ferrero, which I really did think good. Oh but what do all these bloody books matter. I was disappointed but not very much surprised that you gave up your visit.

[*3 lines crossed out*]

I must stand up for myself a bit under the torrent of Gwen's relations. I do want to see somebody really wicked. Are you still wicked, Virginia? I'm so tired of the good. But we had one really nice visit from Eily, who loves you very much you know. Do go & see her some time, it does give her such pleasure.

Then we had an extraordinarily comic visit from Gide whom I hadn't seen for 3 years & who would like me to think him frightfully wicked. We ragged him all the time, gently, just under the surface, but rather maliciously. He couldn't make head or tail of it; & he really was a good deal intrigued about the things which were going on in this house (which *were* rather curious) but I'm sure he got all the cats by the wrong tails. He *is* an old charlatan; though still extraordinarily seductive. And he doesn't know as much about human nature as he imagines.

I could tell you such stories about him... perhaps I will when you come. I think you'd appreciate them, & I have no scruples. We've seen a good deal of Valéry too this winter; who is quite a different sort of bird. (One of the most amusing things was Gide's intense jealousy of our relations with him, & admiration for him & how I poured oil on the fire.) Much more solid altogether. I have never met a man quite so completely disillusioned & disenchanted as he is. I find it very restful in small quantities, & rather stimulating at the same time. He will talk quite endlessly on any subject under the sun. When he doesn't know, he invents. I think those are the best moments. For the rest, life just drifts on. I have just been in bed for 10 days with an infernal sore throat. It's beautifully fine & warm now & the garden is full of orange blossom. Weddings: hum, hum. We do a little bit of honest pimping – in a purely Christian spirit you know – do unto others, etc, – when it comes our way; & it makes me feel dreadfully sentimental, but Hush. We paint a little & eat a little & sleep a *very* little, & read a lot of bad books & think how much more peaceful life is when the house is empty. Do write again soon – Gwen sends her love

Jacques Raverat

The paper Virginia gave to the Society of Heretics in Cambridge was on 'Character in Fiction'. Lady Ottoline Morell, hostess and patroness of the arts, gave fabulous parties at her Oxfordshire house, Garsington Manor, for pacifists, artists and writers.

Monks House,
Rodmell,
Lewes   June 8th 1924

Dear Jacques,

I have left your last long & delicious letter – between you, you write damned good letters, whichever has the credit, the good Darwin or the bad Frog – in my box at home, & so I can't answer your questions. What were they? Perhaps only a general desire to know if I'd seen Eily lately, or Cox, or any of your old flames. I was never in love with Eily. For a time Bernard took my fancy, until I stayed with them, & he talked too much golf – but he writes very well; like Jorrocks; only Englishmen can write like that; so don't you go & try. Will A.F. had another show, & I never went. Isn't it awful? Can one ignore the whole of one side of one's friends' lives, & yet keep on terms of any interest with them? I rather fancy that we're drifting apart – after all, its incredibly difficult to run down to the Land's End, & when Cox is in London, what with she impressing me with her politics, & I her with my literature, we don't get much forrader. Two weeks ago I was in Cambridge, lecturing the Heretics upon Modern Fiction. Do you feel kindly towards

Cambridge? It was, as Lytton would say, rather 'hectic'; young men going in for their triposes; flowering trees on the backs; canoes; fellows' gardens; wading in a slightly unreal beauty; dinners, teas, suppers; a sense, on my part, of extreme age, & tenderness & regret; & so on & so on. We had a good hard headed argument, & I respect the atmosphere, & I'm glad to be out of it. Maynard is very heavy & rather portentous; Maynard is passionately & pathetically in love, because he sees very well that he's dished if he marries her, & she has him by the snout. You can't argue solidly when Lydia's there, & as we set now to the decline, & prefer reason to any amount of high spirits, Lydia's pranks put us all on edge; & Bloomsbury steals off to its dens, leaving Maynard with Lydia on his knee, a sublime but heart rending spectacle.

Please do not repeat this gossip. Lydia came over here the other day & said, 'Please, Leonard, tell me about Mr Ramsay Macdonald. I am seerious – very seerious.' However then she caught a frog & put it in an apple tree; & that's what's so enchanting about her; but can one go through life catching frogs? You should hear Vanessa & Duncan on the subject.

I have had two bloody painful encounters with Middleton Murry; we stuck together at parties like two copulating dogs; but after the first ecstasy, it was boring, disillusioning, flat. The long & short of him is that he's a coward. First he fawns up to me, then when I attack him he plants his dart & runs away. He says we (Bloomsbury) deny our instincts: but why, after all, does writing badly prove that one is morally good?

Children, by Gwen Raverat, wood engraving
(actual size), 1926

Answer me that, my dear Jacques: for I have no room to develop my own arguments. Now he's married a contributor [*Katherine Mansfield*] to the *Adelphi*, and is breeding.

Ottoline – was Ottoline ever a figure or any sort to you? She flaunts about London, not without a certain grandeur, as of a ship with its sails rat eaten, & its masts mouldy, & green sea serpents on the decks. But no image will convey her mixture of humbleness & splendour & hypocrisy. She was shaking powder onto the floor & saying, 'Virginia, why *do* women make up?'

We go back to London tomorrow. Whom do you wish me to see in particular? Do you remember Justin Brooke? A sister of his lived in our house: Morgan Forster's novel [*A Passage to India*] is just out. Do you read him? And what do you think about?

Ever yours

VW

Why not some day send me the family portraits? Children, & all.

Dora Carrington, generally known as Carrington, was living with Lytton Strachey at The Mill House, Tidmarsh, together with her husband Ralph Partridge. The menage moved to Ham Spray House, Hungerford at about this time.

dictated to Gwen Raverat
Vence   7th August 1924

Oh yes my dear Virginia,

I do it quite myself I assure you. *I* think, you know. Gwen just writes (note by GR: I said nothing was too outrageous, & I often did the outrageous bits myself, but Jacques said that bit was in character & I must keep it.) or doesn't write if she thinks I'm getting too outrageous. She is merely my – ah – amanuensis – or – er – scribe. I'm not saying that she can't write a good letter too, but they're quite different.

But there are very few people to whom one can write good letters because they somehow don't react in the right way, even if you like them (the people) quite well when they are there. Perhaps it's a different sort of friendship.

We were both intensely interested in the things you said about Maynard; but I want to know *why* will he be dished if he marries her, & in what particular sense do you mean it? Also, why should he marry her at all? Will she make him? Or is the non-conformist heredity breaking out? I must confess, though it's a thing to be rather ashamed of, that I was also rather pleased, because I've always consid-

94

ered him as a type of the Successful Man; strong (if not silent) with no joints in his armour, (How difficult to sit down) and generally rather inhuman. I suppose I must have been quite wrong; I wish you would write me a little psychological portrait of him, in the manner of La Bruyère. You hardly ever do answer my questions, which is very tiresome of you. There are so many things I want to know. For instance what is the *real* relation between Lytton & Carrington & Mr Partridge? But perhaps it's indiscreet. I've also asked you several times in vain, what you are writing, & what books you read nowadays. There was rather a foolish article about you by ABW in the Times the other day. (Gwen says it was idiotic, but she always is so extreme.) And then I'm always telling you about my wife, & you never tell me anything about your husband. You know I have only met him 2 or 3 times, & I've no idea what he's like really.

I spent most of yesterday reading Mr Shaw's last play, Joan of Arc, & I would say of him as you do of Middleton Murry, (your account of that meeting too was extremely amusing, if somewhat coarsely expressed). Why does writing bad English prove that one is morally good; or even intelligent, I'd add. I still can't understand why people think he's a great man. I wonder what *you* think of him. He seems to me a completely secondrate mind, with only second-hand ideas, or opinions rather. Its rather pathetic to see him discovering the middle ages & writing about the Catholic church, almost as poor old Chesterton might. It would be a joke if he went over. He may have on his age an influence of the same sort as, say, Voltaire, but I cannot believe it will endure. Voltaire has at least the saving (only I'm not sure that it is enough to save him) grace of style; Shaw writes like a preparatory schoolboy, or a Babu. I admit there's a good deal of common sense in his view of Joan, but he leaves out, cold Protestant that he is, all the fierceness of her genius. He never even mentions Péguy in his bibliography; I suppose he's just not quite advanced enough to have heard of him.

But enough of all this, I expect you will scorn me for these opinions. After all opinions (anybody's) are hardly worth writing down; certainly not worth printing. I read also *A Passage to India*, a little time ago. I liked it, & thought it finely written. But I don't know that it's left a very strong impression behind. I go meandering on like this, because it's a hot day & I am lying in the shade of my lime tree with nothing to do till 5 o'clock, when I shall go & paint. I wish you could see this place in the summer. We went right up into the hills last night & came back by moonlight. (Here Jacques says he wants to say it was very beautiful, but can't think how to say it; so *I* say, say *it was very beautiful*, but *he* thinks that's not literary enough for you. However that's the sense. G.R.)

I won't send you the family portraits, flattered though I am that you should ask them. I *wish* you would send me a portrait of yourself, I can hardly remember what you look like – only walking up Tottenham Court Road & carrying daffodils in a very drooping fashion. (by the way why did you say that the world suddenly changed in Dec. 1910 – I

Picking Oranges, by Gwen Raverat, oils, 1924

Cagnes Road (near Vence), by Jacques Raverat, oils, 1923

The Cliffs at Rogerville (near Le Havre), by Jacques Raverat, oils, 1919

Baous des Blancs from Conque, by Jacques Raverat, oils, 1921

should have put it some 6 months later. But why? It didn't really you know.)

But I'm going to do a much more unpardonable thing, which is to send you a copy of two of Elisabeth's poems. You'll see she's nothing if not modern. I think it might amuse you. It reminds me of Rimbaud more than anybody else. Its rather a terrifying prospect isn't it?

Write again soon. We send you both our loves

Jacques

On Seeing Botticelli's Primavera

by Elisabeth Raverat (aged 8 in 1924)

Je l'ai vue
Toute pleine de grace
Tellement elle était belle
C'était le printemps
Et de sa jupe sortaient
Des fleurs qui s'enterraient
Dans ma mere, la terre
    Je l'aime.

Maynard Keynes's brother Geoffrey, married Gwen's sister Margaret on May 12th, 1917.

Monks House,
Rodmell,
Lewes   Sept 4th 1924

My dear Jacques,

   Well, you say I don't answer your questions, so I will sit down with your letter before me & take them, one, two, three.
   1) Why will Maynard be dished if he marries her?
   Because she has the nicest nature in the world & a very limited headpiece. She came to tea on Sunday with your brother in law Geoffrey, & really I had the hardest time in the world. Her conversation is one shriek, two dances; then silence, like a submissive child, with her hands crossed. At 30 this is pathetic. Soon she will be plaintive. And they say you can only talk to Maynard now in words of one syllable. This he will tire of. She will cry, & the great ladies won't ask her to their parties: you old married people can fill it in at your leisure. (I get this largely from other sources)
   2) Why should he marry her? She wants to send her sons to Eton.
   3) I agree that Maynard's fallibility endears him to me.
   4) What is the *real* relation between Lytton, Carrington & Mr P.? Now that's asking, as they say, (unless I have got it wrong) God knows. I imagine a bed has two pillows

Sophie Raverat, by Gwen Raverat, charcoal, 1926?

though, & – but here again I'm quite ignorant, for at our time of life we ignore each their private relations, & find them boring –. Partridge is a bit of a bore; but then what muscles! How he cuts wood, breeds hens, & answers the bell! Carrington is worth twice his salt – but he's a seemly pink firm-fleshed young man, without a doubt. And Lytton of course does not supply *every*thing. I leave this too, to be spelt out.

5) What am I writing? I don't think I shall tell you, because, as you know perfectly well, you don't care a straw what I write; &, like you & Gwen for the matter of that, I'm terrifically egotistic about my writing, think, practi-

99

cally of nothing else, & so, partly from conceit, partly shyness, sensitiveness, what you choose, never mention it, unless someone draws it out with red hot pincers, or like Forster, really takes an interest in my adventures. (however, I've almost finished 2 books [Mrs Dalloway *and* The Common Reader])

6) What do I read? On my table are: Yeats' poems; *Le Bal du Comte d'Orgel* [*by Raymond Radiguet, 1924*]: (which I think very interesting); *Susanne et le Pacifique* [*by Jean Giraudoux, 1921*]: (also interesting); the *Adelphi*; Chaucer; Lord Willoughby de Broke's Autobiography (sporting) [The Sport of our Ancestors, *being a collection of prose and verse setting forth the sport of foxhunting as they knew it, 1921*], a good many Elizabethan plays which I'm going to write about, & – more daily trash: *Joan of Arc*. I can't see why people are moved by this: interested, instructed – yes; but I can't squeeze a tear. I like Shaw as a figure: he seems to me lean, lively, destructive & combative. But Lord! leave me on a desert island with his plays, & I'd rather scale monkey puzzles. But this I've always suffered from. I don't quite trust my self.

7) What is my husband like?

A Jew: very long nosed & thin; immensely energetic; But why I don't talk about *him* is that really you are Anti-semitic, or used to be, when I was in the sensitive stage of engagement; so that it was then impressed upon me not to mention him. I think this was so. And then Gwen, to take up old scandals, said it was high time at my age, I married, & as I was only 3 years older than she, I was hurt, profoundly, & thought you both condescending, flippant, & oh dear, how the Neo-paganism at that stage of my life annoyed me – Every street in Bloomsbury seems now branded with my miseries but I was more than a little mad. I will send you a picture of me done for a vulgar paper called *Vogue* when I get back.

You see, I'm very famous in some circles, *rather* famous, I mean: Americans want to buy my manuscripts. I should like you to have a high opinion of me in this way, & yet – how interesting one's own psychology is – won't talk to you about my writing.

I don't think this is a very nice letter, my dear Jacques, but then you brought it on yourself by asking all those questions; & my style is not good at questions.

By the way, I like your daughter's poems. I don't know how much it is their being French. Everything French has a perfection in my eyes. Anyhow I think them very lovely, very enchanting. May I keep them?

And I don't like my own letters. I don't like the falsity of the relationship – one has to spray an atmosphere round one; yet I do like yours & seem to be able to pierce through your spray, so may you through mine.

Please write soon again. But could you tell me about your painting now? And isn't it the nut, core, kernel (as my Quaker aunt used to call it) of your soul! Gwen don't count compared with your smudges – (excuse what is only literary) does she?

What do you think of Duncan & Vanessa as painters? I should like to know.

Yours VW.

dictated to Gwen Raverat
Vence   [September 1924]

My dear Virginia,

One of the things I find most difficult about writing is that it has to be, essentially, linear. I mean you can only write (or read) one thing at a time; & even memory doesn't alter this fact. Now that's not at all the way my mind works. When you write a word like *Neo Paganism* for instance, it's as if you threw a pebble into a pond. There are splashes in the outer air in every direction, & under the surface waves that follow one another into dark & forgotten corners of my past. You are not only a writer, but a printer & you'll see how difficult it would be to represent this odd phenomenon. One could perhaps, in the middle of a large sheet of paper, write the word NeoPaganism & then radially bits of sentences like this:

Shame at the absurdities of my youth.

Apologies if they really annoyed you.

But almost impossible to believe that you can have taken
    them seriously.

My own annoyance in those days because I fell so short
    of that ideal.

A desire to defend it.

A desire to counterattack.

Etc etc

And all this, you see, simultaneously; though even so it's only what happens on the surface.

My dear Virginia — One of the things I find most difficult about writing is that it has to be, essentially, linear. I mean you can only write (or read) one thing at a time; & even memory doesn't alter this fact. Now that's not at all the way my mind works. When you write a word like Neo Paganism for instance, it's as if you threw a pebble into a pond. There are splashes in the outer air in every direction, & under the surface waves that follow one another into dark & forgotten corners of my past. You are not only a writer, but a printer & you'll see how difficult it would be to represent this odd phenomenon. One could perhaps, in the middle of a large sheet of paper write the word NeoPaganism & then radially bits of sentences like this: Shame at the absurdities of my youth.

Apologies if they really annoyed you.

But almost impossible to believe that you can have taken them so seriously.

My own annoyance in those days, because I fell so short of that ideal.

A desire to defend it.
A desire to counterattack.

&c &c

And all this, you see, simultaneously; though even so it's only what happens on the surface.
Now in painting it's all quite different. But more of that later

Now in painting it's all quite different. But more of that later.

Well, I can easily believe that I must have been, shall we say, a very difficult young man. Very proud & obstinate & umbrageous. But what you call condescension & flippancy was very often only a mask to hide extreme diffidence & fear of seeming ridiculous to you. You never realized, my dear Virginia, how much I admired you. And I beg that you will believe that I say this now in no such spirit (of condescension & flippancy). And you don't realize it now. Or you wouldn't say that I care not a straw about your writing. I can assure you that if I did not I should not so often ask about it. Nor would I have written specially to tell you how much I like *Jacob's Room* & *Monday or Tuesday*. But if you won't tell me, you won't.

You ask about my painting. Well of course. But it's something else as well. The secret is that it's a drug. When life's too bloody & one's friends unbearable, when love has turned to ashes & ambition to dust (wow) there's some that take to drink, or opium, & there's some that turn to God or keep little dogs. Well I paint. When I can paint it's all right & I don't much care about anything else. When I'm too tired to paint or too ill, its hell. It's not, I admit, a very noble Attitude about Art. But there it is. And of course when it does *go*, it's easily the most enduring pleasure of one's life. And, as I was saying, you can see the whole of what you are doing at the same time. And the relations between sky & foreground, feet & hair, nose & navel, are there simultaneously. Surely, when you are writing you are not clearly conscious on Page 259 of what there was on

Page 31. But perhaps that's only because I'm not a writer, & in fact do not naturally think in words. I agree to a certain extent to what you say about letters, & the falsity of the relationship. Though as a matter of fact, even if you don't like your letters, I do. Better I think than almost any that I get nowadays. In spite of the cloud of ink, I suppose that we have a queer sort of image of one another. I wonder what relation it has to our real selves; or if indeed such beings exist at all. Anyhow it's an amusing game.

Do you really think that people of our age & experience of life *can* do anything but play the fool? One has to keep up a certain sort of decency I suppose. One can't be really sincere. At least not in a letter, not in writing. And that brings us round to the beginning again & the too many dimensions. However I don't mind telling you, that I think I should be, as your friend Mr Shaw calls it, better dead. The condition of my life is such that I have not the advantages of either death or life; not of life because I have lost almost every pleasure in the world. Not of death because I am still damnably capable of feeling pain. Please do not repeat this.

By the way did you ever read a dialogue of Paul Valéry called Eupalinos. It contains a good many of the things I believe on life & death & art & the body. I find it extraordinarily moving, & most profoundly true.

To return again to our past of 12 or more years ago. It's very inconvenient you should remember so many things about it. How did you ever know that I was an anti-semite for instance? I don't think I ever saw you when you were

engaged, & certainly not since you were married. It's true in this way that I've very often found that things and people that I disliked were Jewish; but I did make friends rather intimately with one Jew in Paris years ago; & I always wanted to know your husband better, (I do like *some* Jews), though I dare say we should have disagreed in most of our opinions; but that doesn't count much.

I am surprised that you should say that you find that people's private relations are boring. Talking to fools of course is boring always, but otherwise I still find them, I mean personal relations, much too interesting. They can be tragic or farcical or devastating or ecstatic & half a hundred other things (Gwen's in a hurry). But never never boring. Always I think rather dangerous, because whatever resolution one has not to go beneath the surface one's always being drawn into intimacies & giving oneself away, but perhaps it doesn't matter really.

I do wish you'd get into an aeroplane & come over & see us soon. If I could move I'd come to England & talk to you for two nights & one day & then come back to Vence. It's really a very easy journey you know & I'll meet you with my car when you like at Antibes or Nice.

I'm made to feel in no doubtful manner that I'd better stop, so I'll send you my love & say goodbye & Gwen says she will write you a separate & independent letter one of these days.

Yrs J.R.

Note: that's because he objects to my drawing squiggle-wiggles on the blotting paper while I wait. It's not fair. GR.

P.S. by Jacques. You ask what I think of Vanessa & Duncan as painters. To tell the truth I hardly know; I don't think I've seen any of Vanessa's work for about 10 years & none of Duncan's since his exhibition in 1920 [*his first one-man show*]. I've no notion what sort of things they are painting nowadays. I have for a long time been rather bewildered at the varieties of Duncan's style, & the ease with which he changed from one to the other. Which is the real Duncan? I haven't the faintest idea?

I've been trying to buy Valéry in London, & am told he is out of print. Can you tell me how I could get his dialogues?

Monks House,
Rodmell   Oct. 3rd 1924

My dear Jacques,

Certainly the painters have a great gift of expression. A highly intelligent account you seem to me to give of the processes of your own mind when I throw Neo Paganism in. In fact I rather think you've broached some of the problems of the writer's too, who are trying to catch & consolidate & consummate (whatever the word is for making literature) those splashes of yours; for the falsity of the past (by which I mean Bennett, Galsworthy & so on) is precisely I think that they adhere to a formal railway line of sentence, for its convenience, never reflecting that people don't & never did feel or think or dream for a second in that way; but all over the place, in your way.

I'm writing now, partly because I was so much intrigued by your letter, & felt more in touch, partly because this is my last evening of peace. I go back to London tomorrow. Then there'll be people upon people; & I shall dash in & out, & go to concerts, & make engagements, & regret making engagements. The difficulty of writing letters is, for one thing, that one has to simplify so much, & hasn't the courage to dwell on the small catastrophes which are of such huge interest to oneself; & thus has to put on a kind of unreal personality; which, when I write to you for example, whom I've not seen these 11 years, becomes inevitably jocular. I suppose joviality is a convenient mask; & then, being a writer, masks irk me; I want, in my old age, to have done with all superfluities, & form words precisely on top of the waves of my own mind – a formidable undertaking.

About your letter, however; I didn't mean that private relations bore me: which is indeed an intolerable perversion of my real meaning, who find relations of all kinds more & more engrossing, & (in spite of being made a fool of so often by one's impulse to surrender everything – dignity & propriety – to intimacy) final, in some way; enduring; gigantic; & beautiful. Indeed, I find all this in my relations with people, & what I can guess of theirs. What I meant was that *sexual* relations bore me more than they used: am I a prude? Am I feminine? Anyhow, for two years past, I have been a spectator of I daresay a dozen affairs of the heart – violent & crucial; & came to the conclusion that love is a disease; a frenzy; an epidemic; oh but how dull, how monotonous, & reducing its young men & women to what abysses of mediocrity! It's true that all my lovers were of the simplest type; & could only flush & fade crudely like sea anemones bathed now blue, now red. Thats what I meant, I think.

Our loves, yours & mine & that granite monolithic Gwen's – (until she writes to me, I shall say what I like of her to her husband) were of a very different kind. But then we were creatures of temperament. No: your admiration

Jacques ill in bed, by Gwen Raverat, ink, 1924

of me was not apparent; but then I was alarmed of your big nose, your bright eyes, your talking French, & your having such a quick easy way with you, as if you had solved the problems of life, – gone straight into the middle of the honeycomb without one miss. Yes – that's how I figure you: that's still (vaguely now) the image I have of my dear & adorable Jacques – but I should never have dared call him so to his face. And then, (this is a secret) for some reason, your & Gwen's engagement, & being in love, took on for me a symbolic character; which I even tried to put down in writing. All very absurd I suppose: still you were very much in love, & it had an ecstatic quality. Indeed, you will laugh, but I used to think of you, in a purely literary way, as the two people who represented that passion in my mind; & still, when I think of you, I take out my brush, & paint both of your faces a divine sunset red. How oddly composed are one's feelings! You would never have guessed, I daresay, that Jacques & Gwen always appear to Virginia in a sunset glow?

As for gossip, I hope to collect some in the great world.

Vanessa is getting a little querulous about Maynard & Lydia, & will have, she says, to turn out. Our Mrs Joad [*Marjorie Thompson*] has left her Mr Joad. Our Dadie is a very nice boy [*George 'Dadie' Rylands who was assisting with the* Hogarth Press]. Our Karin Stephen sent me to bed with a violent headache last week, & ruined the last pages of my novel (oh yes, I'll write another letter & tell you about my writing – anything you want to know). She descended on us, & God knows I like her; but there's a deafness of the spirit about her, which exhausts more than dragging a ton of coal upstairs: so hearty she is, good humoured, & right minded. The poor devil interests me for having tried to live with Adrian, & for being inarticulately aware of her own obtuseness. She can't feel; she can't enjoy; she can't be intimate; she cares for nothing. Yet she has the most perfect apparatus for life in body & head & wealth & freedom. To cure herself she pays £1 daily to a psycho-analyst; & would, she told me, prefer to be entirely destitute could she only feel things, instead of being as she is now, non-feeling. But this may convey nothing to you.

However, I'm awfully shy of saying how really & truly I would do a great deal to please you & can only very very dimly murmur a kind of faint sympathy & love.

Yrs

VW

Vence   [early October 1924]

My dear Virginia,

I meant to write to apologize to you at once when your letter (the one before the last) came; but I kept putting it off, thinking that as I'd waited for 12 or 13 years before apologising, a day or two more wouldn't matter. I apologise for the remark of mine you quoted (which I'd quite forgotten.) Lord, how arrogant & absurd. I *do* agree with you that Neo Paganism must have been very irritating; only I should have thought it was still more ridiculous. In fact I never (even then) imagined that you could look at it in any other way – It surprises me to hear that you took it seriously at all.

Anyhow it's all over long ago; it died in 1914 I should think, though it was sick before – Neo Pagans, where are they? Here's Jacques & me very old in Vence, & Ka so pathetic & lost in Cornwall; & do the Oliviers exist or not? Frances I believe carries on the tradition in the fields of Cambridge – at least as far as neo-paganism can be combined with evangelical christianity, (which I think any one but Frances would find difficult.) And all the others are dead or have quarrelled or gone mad or are making a lot of money in business. It doesn't seem to have been a really successful religion, though it was very good fun while it lasted.

And what about Bloomsburyism? From here the front looks still firm; but is it solid behind? Is it only a front,

Elisabeth, Gwen and Sophie Raverat c. 1923

concealing earthquakes & chasms? You must tell me.

For I'm coming to London next week (say about 14th Tuesday.) I've not been away from Vence for more than 2 years & I am very moth-eaten & damp in the mind & don't feel very sure of my manners – I'm to have a holiday & see the world.

Can I come & see you? I'll bring the Valéry. Write to me at the young Keyneses: 10 Boundary Rd, St Johns Wood

I do want to see you.

I want to see Everybody.

Yrs Gwen R

FROM JACQUES RAVERAT TO VIRGINIA WOOLF
added to previous letter from GR

dictated to Gwen Raverat

My dear Virginia

As I cannot come myself I will next week send Gwen to you with *Eupalinos*. Please don't lose it, it's my only copy. This is just to say that your most touching & adorable letter came last night; it sent a glow of warmth & pleasure through my old & frozen bones. Thank you dear Virginia, it was lovely of you to write so.

Yrs Jacques

PS I will write a long letter when Gwen comes back to me. Please don't read *Eupalinos* as a summary of my beliefs: only it does put some things rather well.

FROM VIRGINIA WOOLF'S DIARY

Friday 17th October 1924

Heres poor old Jacques writing to me, & Gwen wants to come & see me, after 11 years: a relationship revived by the art of the pen, across France. I rather dread revivals: partly vanity; you're fatter, less beautiful; changed; so self-conscious [?] am I; & then – the effort. Seeing people, now I see them so easily, is an effort. Why –

Boules, by Gwen Raverat, wood engraving (reduced in size), c. 1924

dictated to Gwen Raverat
Vence   12th November 1924

My dear Virginia

I know it's my turn, but I'm not going to write you a long letter tonight; I'm only going to write to get a letter out of you; because the day after Gwen left for England I fell ill, & I've been ill ever since. They call it cystitis, it's in the bladder & most infernally painful. So you will understand that after 5 weeks of it, I'm scarcely in a state of mind to write you an intelligent letter. Nearly all the time I can think of nothing but my bladder, which is, you will admit, rather degrading. But the last 3 or 4 days I've been feeling a bit more human, & beginning to think about things again. I want to write volumes in answer to your last letter, about me & Gwen & love in general. But not tonight.

I must tell you however, that being too weak to paint, I have actually started to write. This will make you laugh after all my protests against literature. I tried a book in English, but it wouldn't do at all. I don't understand the language, & I feel that all the words & phrases are stale & lifeless; but I am going ahead famously with my Memoirs in French. [*They did not get beyond his boyhood experiences at Bedales.*] It seems to come straight & direct & easy after the self conscious-ness of the beginning. It's all about my first adventures in England at the age of 13; I don't suppose it will amuse any-one else, but anyhow it passes the time till I can paint again.

I was tremendously interested by Gwen's account of her
visit to you; I wish she had not been called back & could
have seen you again. It made me more than ever want to
see you. Meanwhile do remember that I am at present very
dependent on the letters of my friends. They help to keep
me human not a mere amorphous invalid. So do write to
me soon, & I will try again as soon as my brain gets a little
clearer.

Yrs Jacques Raverat

P.S. from Gwen
Jacques has been very ill & we rather thought he was
going to die, but he's better now I think – till next time –

He didn't tell me he was ill, till I found out by mistake, but he was very bad when I got back here. It was fun being in England, I felt quite young again.

I forgot to ask, that young man you keep in the cellar (not the one that was at tea) *he's* a neopagan, isn't he?

Sitting with Jacques (the woman is probably Babette Giroux),
by Gwen Raverat, pencil, 1924

Dorothy was the older sister of Lytton Strachey and was married to the French painter, Simon Bussy.

52 Tavistock Square, W.C.1   Nov. 29th 1924

My dear Dorothy,

... I had a visit from Gwen the other day, very tragic I thought, and I half intend to go and see them, in which case I shall sponge a tea off you. Last night Pippa [*Strachey*] looked in, entirely resembling a nice small dancing bear. She danced once round the room on her hind legs and went off to the ballet. Marjorie [*Strachey*] continues to develop the soundest and ripest character in Bloomsbury; in short, all Stracheys are doing well. Adrian and Karin are still separate; Leonard and I continue married.

That is all

Yrs V.W.

Tavistock Square
London
W.C.1.
Telephone: Museum 2621

Nov 29ᵗʰ 1924

My dear Jacques,

I am much distressed, not figuratively but
genuinely, to hear what a horror of a time you have
been having. It was tantalising to see old Gwen
for such a second, but the best of these drawings
is that they are cut out of the rock, & their
take is enough to convince one how immense is
their solidity (to which Gwen has added; & taught,
some vein of wisdom, & sweetness of temper which
I rather envy her — I like seeing women
weather the world so well)
But what am I to do with your copy of the Revue
Francaise? I don't like to trust it to the
post, which has lost me my Proust memorial
volume this year. Who is going out to you next?
Tell me, & I'll send it. I hope to read
Valéry again. My first reading rather baffled:

Lady Colefax was married to a dull Yorkshire MP who provided her with her title and money. She entertained in the beautiful 18th century Argyll House in the King's Road where literati mingled with diplomats and Hollywood stars. She began to pursue Virginia in 1922.

52 Tavistock Square,
London WC1   Nov 29th 1924

My dear Jacques,

I am much distressed, not figuratively but genuinely, to hear what a horror of a time you have been having. It was tantalizing to see old Gwen for such a second, but the best of these Darwins is that they are cut out of the rock, & three taps is enough to convince one how immense is their solidity (to which Gwen has added; I thought, some vein of wisdom, & sweetness of temper which I rather envy her – I like seeing women weather the world so well).

But what am I to do with your copy of the *Revue Française*? I don't like to trust it to the post, which has lost me my Proust memorial volume this year. Who is going out to you next? Tell me, & I'll send it. I hope to read Valéry again. My first reading rather baffled: I felt an odd emptiness, conformity of some kind, triteness, I even go so far as to add; beneath the beauty & brilliancy of the surface. I felt I'd read it before, not so well set out. But I don't trust myself reading French: lately I've had one or two disappointments, expecting more from the manner than I got in the end; so

I must read this again. You French are fundamentally so damned logical, & this freezes the soul in one or two of its veins.

What were the questions I had to answer? About the young man in the basement – George Rylands. Alas, he will soon cease to be in the basement, King's College requiring him to work harder at his dissertation, & so he will be going after Xmas to write upon Diction in Poetry, & so win a fellowship, & live at Cambridge & teach, which they now insist on – rather a nuisance for us. It makes it necessary to reorganize our staff, take in a new partner, engage a new secretary & so on: but I won't bore you with domestic details. Hours & hours of our time go in discussions & interviews. He is a semi-NeoPagan perhaps. At King's they are all reminded of Rupert – partly his yellow hair, partly his poetry, which is not so good as Rupert's. He is a very charming spoilt boy, sprung of the rich who have no money, & so rather dazzled by London & parties, & perhaps he scents himself; but at heart he is uncorrupted, (so I think, others disagree) & all young & old vile men, like Eddie Marsh & so on, fall in love with him, & he dines out every night, & treats his lovers abominably. However, if he don't get his fellowship, he will come back here, if possible. A life at Cambridge teaching seems to me a skeleton life; but then, it has to be.

One reflection occurred to me, dealing with our Mrs Joad, the other basement dweller – how much nicer young women are than young men. I hope to get a rise out of you. Nicer, I say, humaner, less conceited, more sensitive,

124

– not cleverer. But a man has to be very clever to balance what my dear Jacques I can only call his damned offensive good opinion of himself – & of his sex.

Now please tell me about your autobiography, which so whets my curiosity that I must entreat you to let me see it. If I translated it, couldn't we publish it?

Please write it with a view to this, & let it be the waste paper basket, conduit pipe, cess pool, treasure house, & larder & pantry & drawing & dining & bed room of your existence. Write about everything, without order, or care. Being a Frog, you won't of course; you will organize & compose. Still, let me see it, & get on with it.

It is awful how business runs away with one's time. Soon I shall have to describe a fresh set of people to you – a man called Angus Davidson, who thinks of coming to us. Then, socially, what about Lady Colefax? Being the most successful, hardest mouthed hostess in London, she retains spots about the size of a sixpenny piece, of astonishing sensibility on her person. Having left her umbrella here, I, in malice or sport, proceeded to describe it, glowing & gleaming among my old gamps. Whereupon this hard bitten old hostess of 50 flushed quite red, & said, 'Mrs Woolf, I know what you think of my umbrella – a cheap, stubby, vulgar umbrella, you think my umbrella; & you think I have a bag like it – a cheap flashy bag covered with bad embroidery.' And it was too true. Only, if she saw it, must there not be depths in Lady Colefax? Think this out, & let me know. Please write & say how you are.

Yrs, VW

Steuart Wilson was the brother of Jacques's Cambridge friend Hugh. Well known as a tenor singer, his consistent high spirits covered the financial anxiety of being a performer. When he was ill that year with an ulcer, Jacques sent money via a mutual friend.

dictated to Gwen Raverat
first sheet missing

[December 1924]

... when one's quite grown up and French and living in the 20th century one has to paint from nature. Is there anything really possible between pure fairy tales & history? But that would take us too far tonight I think. And anyhow you'd quote at once a dozen examples to confute me. But all this has a bearing too on what you said in an earlier letter about your view all those years ago, of me & of Gwen & of our falling in love & of our marriage. To simplify things: I have a certain fairly constant view of my own character; and there is another opinion of me which is held by a number of other people; & the two don't coincide in the least. How the devil is one to know what the truth about character is under those conditions? (I hope the other people are right.) But enough of all this vague & abstract stuff. You'll perceive I'm still rather muddle-headed. But I know clearly enough one thing I want to say & that is that your letters, particularly the last 3 or 4, have given me something, which very few people have been able to give me, in these last years. It is so extraordinarily nice of you to write to me like that in the middle of all the business & the fullness of your life in London, & I just wanted to say thank you.

Sometimes I think what fun it would be to plunge into the world again – people & parties & all that, & I'm filled with black (or green is it?) jealousy of all you people who can go about & do things. You see I'm shewing you a little of the more ignoble side of my character, but I somehow think you'll understand.

I did like the photographs you sent too. It seems to me you look younger than I remembered, and perfectly enchanting. The only person I've seen for months is Steuart Wilson. Do you know him? He is learning to sing with De Retzke in Nice, & he comes up here & sings to us occasionally; very well indeed to my mind. He is the most bracing person I've ever met, like high mountain air, so that its almost impossible not to fall in love with him. Most people do. He's always happy, he talks incessantly in that queer Wilson-Worcester nearly clerical voice; he enjoys everything & everybody (how far this goes I don't know) & is entirely mysterious to me. I get no glimpse of what there is behind all those high spirits, & I can hardly believe that anyone is really as happy as that all the time.

What's this about Angus Davidson [*the Woolf's new assistant at the* Hogarth Press]? I don't know him, but I know his brother Malcolm also a singer & a composer of rather an ordinary sort. His legs are so short that Babette refuses to go for walks with him, but they might look very fine in a kilt. His jaws stick out monstrously below his ears, & he's wonderfully well pleased with himself all round.

Jacques ill in bed, by Gwen Raverat, pencil, c.1924

Scotch of course.
Do write again when you've time –
I send you my love
Yrs
Jacques Raverat

PS You won't get a rise out of me about young women
& young men; I'm beginning to doubt whether you may
not be right after all – at least not such *very* young women,
but women of 40 or thereabouts.

The Baous with Bathing Figures, by Jacques Raverat, oils, 1923

Olive Tree at Villa Adèle, by Jacques Raverat, oils, 1923

Portrait of Jacques Raverat, Gwen Raverat, oils, 1924

Vita Sackville-West met the Woolfs – indeed Bloomsbury – for the first time at the end of 1922. By the time this letter was written her love affair with Virginia had got to the stage of serious flirtation. Gwen's view of Roger Fry's art differed from Virginia's – Gwen believed he had 'a quality of sensitiveness'.

Monks House,
Rodmell   Dec. 26th 1924

My dear Jacques,

Do not expect wit or sense in this letter, only the affection of a drugged & torpid mind. Oh an English Christmas! We are not Christians; we are not social; we have no part in the fabric of the world, but, all the same, Christmas flattens us out like a steam roller; turkey, pudding, tips, waits, holly, good wishes, presents, sweets; so here we sit, on Boxing day, at Rodmell, over a wood fire, & I can only rouse myself by thinking of you. In particular. I want to know 1) how you are. 2) Whether you are getting on with your autobiography; 3) What you are thinking; 4) what feeling; 5) what imagining, criticizing, seeing – do catch that wild woman Gwen & stick a pen in her paw.

All that I predicted about Maynard & Lydia is coming to pass. They dined with us 2 nights ago: & my God! the poor sparrow is already turning into a discreet, silent, serious, motherly, respectable, fowl, with eggs, feathers, cluck cluck clucking all complete. A melancholy sight indeed, & I foresee the day when she dislikes any reference to dancing.

Maynard is – But enough of the Keynes', as they are called in Bloomsbury. 'Mr Keynes has very bad taste,' my cook said to me, after the dinner. 'Madame laughs, & he is so serious.' Soon Vanessa is escorting her to the divorce court. Once divorced, she will give up dancing. But enough of the Keynes.

Now who shall we pitch on? Casting a shadow over my paper at the present moment is the fine oriental head of Angus Davidson. He is staying here to know us & be known (he is our partner now) &, despite his brother's neck, I like him very much; & think him likely to be our salvation – gentle, considerate, cautious, kind, with a mind smooth & sensitive as the thickest cream. Do you know that quality in young well-bred Englishmen? Slightly hesitating, diffident, & unselfconscious. He is working in cross-stitch at a design by Duncan for a chair; Leonard is ordering onions from a catalogue. Who should come in, the other day, but our Will [*Arnold Forster*]; more stretched, pinched, parchmenty than ever; squeaking with goodness; & as nice as can be, but why will Ka always introduce him in a letter calling attention to the wildness & ferocity of his genius: whereupon one hears a squeak on the stairs & in runs Will. 'Little Wully's by way of being a painter' he said at tea, I urging him, with my notorious lack of consideration, to write books, either about roses, or about the League of Nations, which to tell the truth is far more his line than perpetually worrying the finest crow quills over the Apennines – or whatever that eternal picture of his may be. But enough of the Coxes.

Who is there next? Well, only a high aristocrat called Vita Sackville-West, daughter of Lord Sackville, daughter of Knole, wife of Harold Nicholson, & novelist; but her real claim to consideration, is, if I may be so coarse, her legs. Oh they are exquisite – running like slender pillars up into her trunk, which is that of a breathless cuirassier (yet she has 2 children) but all about her is virginal, savage, patrician; & why she writes, which she does with complete competency, & a pen of brass, is a puzzle to me. If I were she, I should merely stride, with 11 elk hounds, behind me, through my ancestral woods. She descends from Dorset, Buckingham, Sir Philip Sidney, & the whole of English history, which she keeps, stretched in coffins, one after another, from 1300 to the present day, under her dining room floor. But you, poor Frog, care nothing for all this.

Roger Fry is getting a little grumpy. He is not, you see, (or I imagine you see) a born painter, & this impediment seems to obstruct the run of his sympathies, so that he makes no allowances, but judges the imperfect & frail purely as if he were still an impeccable undergraduate, an incorruptible Apostle: whereas for my part I grow more mellow every day.

There! I think I will leave off with that tribute to myself. Love from everybody in the room.

Yours affectionately VW

It is said that the *Adelphi* is coming to an end. We go back to London next Saturday.

France 1925

Virginia had contributed a few pieces to Vogue *under the editorship of Dorothy Todd, who called on other Bloomsbury stalwarts for articles and reviews. Logan Pearsall Smith criticised Virginia for this by writing that he: 'grieved to see Bloomsbury descend from the heights & scatter its pearls in Mayfair'.*

52 Tavistock Square,
London   Jan 24th 1925

My dear Jacques,

   As I was eating my muffin in bed this morning in came an exquisite crate from the South of France filled with flowers of every colour & smell, which I frantically tumbled on the bed to see who could have sent them, & there was your card! I assure you it brought the tears to these hardened eyes of mine, that *you* should have thought of me. And I was just writing to you (a thing I enjoy doing thoroughly, for I write to no one else now) to say that if you'd really like it, I'll send out the proofs of my novel [*Mrs Dalloway*], which has just arrived, on condition you don't bother to write to me about it, or even read it; & *don't mention* it to anyone for fear we should be asked for it, & it won't be out till May. For no other human being in the world would I do this – why, I don't know. But I'm a little morbid about people reading my books.

   I was seeing Roger Fry last night, & he said, talking of you, that he thought your work getting more & more interesting, & wanted to see it, & wished me to tell you this,

& would like to write to you about it himself, but perhaps he won't, so I do instead. What he said was that he thought it extraordinary how you had put aside the things likely to lead to success, & gone on your own lines, so that he thought your last work infinitely better than your early. His praise about painting always seems to me the best worth having, not that one agrees with him, but that his honesty is so incorruptible, & his perceptions so fine. Tell me if there is anything more particular I can ask him. When people praise my writing I want to know why. Anyhow he praised your painting very highly.

I've been engaged in a great wrangle with an old American called Pearsall Smith on the ethics of writing articles at high rates for fashion papers like *Vogue*. He says it demeans one. He says one must write only for the *Lit. Supplement* & the *Nation* & Robert Bridges & prestige & posterity & to set a high example. I say Bunkum. Ladies clothes & aristocrats playing golf don't affect my style; & they would do his a world of good. Oh these Americans! How they always muddle everything up! What he wants is prestige: what I want, money. Now my dear sharp pointed & Gallic Jacques, please decide between us.

Then I have seen our Ka, in her mother-in-laws grey suit & set of furs, a perfect specimen of solid county life, out-wardly; but inwardly, much as usual; that is rather flustered & affectionate, & troubled, it seems to me, about her past; & life's discrepancies, very wise in her own way, which is not *our* way. She has no feeling whatever for the arts. This is the greatest barrier of all, I believe. You & I can chatter like a whole parrot house of cockatoos (such is my feeling) because we have the same language at heart: but with Ka, one looks across a wall. Whether what one says reaches her I doubt. But these barriers have their fascination. Only for living with, they're impossible.

You ask me about Mrs. Joad [*Marjorie Thompson*] – truth to tell, she is rather a problem. The younger generation, I suppose one ought to say; but I don't much believe in these distinctions. She is a tall, straight shingled woman of 25. Came to London, School of Economics, read Shaw, thought she ought to live with a man; did; took up with a clever little bounder called Joad; lived with him; married him; found a letter from a woman in a drawer; left him; now has a room of her own, & walks out with various Cambridge young men, who are not entirely devoted to the foible of loving their own sex. Now comes the point. Being thus, one would have thought emancipated to the verge of dissolution, she won't let Joad divorce her. Him she wishes to divorce. But why does respect for convention suddenly assert itself here? Anyhow, she is without illusions, & faithful as these young women are; fiery; on her dignity, & quite capable of biting the end of Angus' nose off, if he should put upon her, which God knows, Angus is the last man to do. She quarrelled all day with Dadie (the fair young man Gwen saw in the basement) but has, I think, affection & respect for the old Woolves – the male wolf anyhow.

Have you any views on loving one's own sex? All the young men are so inclined, & I can't help finding it mildly foolish; though I have no particular reason. For one thing, all the young men tend to the pretty & ladylike, for some reason, at the moment. They paint & powder, which wasn't the style in our day at Cambridge. I think it does imply some clingingness – a tiny lap dog, called Sackville West, came to see me the other day (a cousin of my aristocrats, & will inherit Knole) & my cook said, who was the lady in the drawing room? He has a voice like a girl's, & a face like a persian cat's, all white & serious, with large violet eyes & fluffy cheeks. Well, you can't respect the amours of a creature like that. Then the ladies, either in self protection, or imitation or genuinely, are given to their sex too. My aristocrat (ah, but I have now 2 or 3, whom I'll tell you about – they interest me) is violently Sapphic, & contracted such a passion for a woman cousin, that they fled to the Tyrol, & some mountainous retreat together, to be followed in an aeroplane by a brace of husbands. [*In fact Violet Trefusis, with whom Vita eloped, was not a cousin, but a childhood friend. In 1920, Harold Nicolson and Denys Trefusis caught up with them in Amiens, persuading them to come home.*] The mothers of girls are said to take it to heart. I can't take either of these aberrations seriously. To tell you a secret, I want to incite my lady to elope with me next. Then I'll drop down on you & tell you all about it.

Karin Stephen is giving a party with me; so on the 4th of Feb. think of me with commiseration & affection. For it's all my damned sentimental desire to be of use to the afflicted that's to blame. (Note: I've just been involved in another affair of the kind with the poet Eliot, & Leonard says it is positively disgusting – this trait in me – pure vanity. Now is it?) She is imprisoned in a kind of fastness of callousness; can't feel, or hate, or enjoy; & has a purely fictitious idea that if only she could see people, in crowds, constantly, but never alone, for she dreads intimacy, she would be cheered & made like other people. So once a month there is to be a party – & each party is to be mothered by Karin & one other lady – & each will be a ghastly failure, & she will fling herself on her bed in tears. Halfway through every evening, the vanity of life dawns upon her; & she despairs. It is a curious case, & she suffers, I believe, tortures.

Well, this is all very rambling; merely a gossip & I don't suppose you realise in the least how the flowers coming from you, on the eve of my birthday too, pleased me. There they are, against my painted walls, great bouquets of yellow & red & pink. They rather remind me of all your quips & cranks, & sitting by the river at the Grange, when you made me smoke one of Sir George's cigars – & I so much wanted you to admire me, & thought I was a desolate old stick compared with the younger generation. But now we are back at the Neo Pagans; & then there's a great deal to be said, which I shall continue in a few days.

Let me see your memoirs, & send any scraps of a letter you like to dictate to that dear old creature Gwen.

Yrs ever

VW

Wednesday [28th January 1925]

My dear Virginia,

How lovely to get such a long letter from you. Jacques isn't quite well enough to write himself today, but he's going to write very soon; & he wants to say that he would like nothing better than the proofs of your novel & feels it a great honour to be allowed to see them. So do please send them soon; & send them by *Registered Book Post, printed matter Imprimé Récommandé; ends of the parcel undone; & not sealed with wax.* Believe me this is of immense importance; if it gets into the clutches of the Parcel Post it will take 3 months to get here, or else never at all. Don't let a menial send it off. I wouldn't trust anyone but Leonard to do it. – He goes on eating nothing & it seems to make no difference; sometimes – every 3 or 4 days or so – he has a mouthful of Benger's Food! & says how nasty it is; & then he dreams of banquets at night.

Dearest Virginia, you don't know how nice it is of you to write so often.

Yrs
Gwen

Jacques was becoming very ill. Other than a little Bengers Food, he had stopped eating. Gwen's sister Margaret visited, with her husband Geoffrey Keynes. 'It is such a relief to be able to speak straight out about death as an ordinary thing, instead of having to listen to the vague doctor-jargon of the man here; who will pretend J is getting better,' Gwen wrote to Ka of the Keynes's visit. Gwen made two haunting wood engravings of Jacques at this time (pages 143 & 150).

dictated to Gwen Raverat
Villa Adèle,
Vence A.M.   [January 1925]

My dear Virginia,

What searching questions. Do you expect true answers? The whole truth would be much too long for a letter. Anyhow I don't know the whole truth, & certainly I wouldn't tell it you; but I'll tell you parts if you like. What I am thinking about: food. I have been living for a fortnight on morphine & a little sugar. I have lost all hunger or appetite or desire to eat. But I keep thinking about things I have eaten & how good they were, from plain beans & bacon to the most elaborate civet. And wine too. Perhaps after all greed is the dominant vice in my character.

What I am feeling: bored & sleepy & very tired. I haven't the energy or the desire or the impulse left to start any new work; to write even a letter is an immense effort, & you mustn't expect too much of me. About my memoirs: I've more or less finished off the first part of them, from about 13 to 16. I very much doubt whether any more will ever be written; though I should have liked, in a way, to write about Cambridge & Rupert & London & all that time. I have always thought it would be extremely interesting to write a true narrative of his amours with Ka. Lord, what a mess they made of it. But it would mean months of work. There are a lot of other true stories too, that seem to me far stranger, than anything one could invent. Any novel I mean. But of course they couldn't be published for a hundred years.

I've been looking over my pictures; there's about a dozen or so that I'm rather proud of. They're really rather good, let me tell you. I found a nude that I painted 3 months ago & had almost forgotten during my illness. It quite startled me. It's as good as ... as good as ... And now I suppose I shan't ever paint any more, just as I was beginning to find out what I was & what I wanted. I do like the little pictures of people you send in your letters. Particularly the one of the Aristocratic Lady – Sackville West, was it? I don't know the aristocratic but I know the type & I know the legs. And of course you know the proverb: 'Once a virgin, always a virgin.' And it doesn't seem to matter how many husbands or lovers or children you have. And who & what is Mrs Joad? I read Eothen the other day. It *was* still possible to write English prose in 1840 [*Originally published in 1844, Alexander William Kinglake's book was still famous*]. What's the matter with it now? I've been thinking about it, because I've been planning a novel in English which I shall never write but perhaps Gwen may (No no no G.) about the true

142

Jacques Raverat, by Gwen Raverat,
wood engraving (actual size), 1925

story & character of Andre Gide. One could so easily trans-
late it to Cambridge say, & that would make it much less
unpublishable. Though what the police would say ... Goodbye dear Virginia. Write again *soon*.

I send you my love. J.R.

P.S. Please I want to buy your novel & book of criticism.
Send them as soon as you can –

P.S. Thank God for morphine anyhow.

Mary Hutchinson, a.k.a Mary Hutch, Bloomsbury beauty, was a first cousin once removed of Lytton Strachey and married to St John Hutchinson. She was Clive Bell's mistress up till 1927 and sometimes flirted with Virginia.

52 Tavistock Square   Feb 5th 1925

My dear Jacques,

   I was struck down with influenza the very day I wrote to you, & am still in bed. Otherwise I should have sent off my proofs, before, but they were muddled up, & influenza makes me like a wet dish cloth – even to sort them was beyond me. I have left them uncorrected. Much has been rewritten. Do a little re-writing on my behalf. Anyhow, don't cast me from you; & say nothing, or anything, as you like. (It will be sent tomorrow, 6th.)

   Being bedridden, my view of the world has had a great thumb put over it. I can't think how you keep so sharp & clear. I have seen Clive Bell, who gave me another headache; he is a good fellow, however. I was so rash as to tell him he praised his Polly Flinders too much – his pretty Poll – his paramour – his Mary Hutch, I mean. (I forget if you are aware of that highly respectable alliance, which is far more lasting & punctiliously observed than any marriage.) I said he should not be praising her legs in company, or cracking up at her little witticisms, or even repeating the tributes of other gentlemen. But, he said, he did it to show Vanessa that she is a serious human being. He said, just because Mary

Under the Lime Tree, by Gwen Raverat, oils, 1923

Elisabeth Raverat, by Jacques Raverat, oils, 1923

dresses well, & you & Nessa badly, you think her dull: so I must prove to you how silly you both are.

Clive is now shaped like a spade & thick as an oak tree. He wears bright blue socks, which he is for ever hitching up, & his trousers, for some reason which a man may know, are always above his knees. But how good hearted he is – bunches of grapes arrive for me; & yet I never do anything but bite his nose off when I see him, & laugh at him behind his back. I have an idea you & Gwen hated him. Let me assure you, you were wrong. Not that I claim for him any of the heroic virtues. Being bred a Puritan, (in the main – but I had a French greatgrandmother to muddle me) I warm my hands at these red-hot-coal men. I often wish I had married a fox hunter. It is partly the desire to share in life somehow, which is denied to us writers. Is it to you painters? Ever since I was a child I have envied people who did things – But even influenza shall not mislead me into egotistical autobiographical revelations – of course, I long to talk to you about myself, my character, my writings, but I am witheld – by what?

Karin's party came off last night, & I lay in bed & imagined it all very brilliant. Leonard put on his deceased brother in law's (who died in a bath at Eastbourne) dress clothes, & went off to brew the punch. Hope Mirrlees arrived half an hour early (do you admire her novels? – I can't get an ounce of joy from them, but like seeing her & Jane billing & cooing together).

Then came 40 young Oxford men, & three very pretty girls; Vanessa, Mary Hutch; Clive & Lytton – Lytton gravitated to the 40 young men, & was heard booming & humming from flower to flower. Vanessa, who had not dressed, sat commandingly on a sofa, talking to a sculptor called Tomlin, & to no one else, for she is beyond the pale now, makes no attempt to conciliate society, & often shocks me by her complete indifference to all my floating loves & jealousies – but with such a life, packed like a cabinet of drawers – Duncan, children, painting, Roger – how can she budge an inch or find a cranny of room for anyone? Clive came in late, having been dining with Mary at her new house in Regents Park. She has a ships steward to serve at table, & whether for this reason or another, provides the most spicy liquors, foods, cocktails, & so on – for example, an enormous earthenware dish, last time I was there, garnished with every vegetable, in January – peas, greens, mushrooms, potatoes; & in the middle the tenderest cutlets, all brewed in a sweet stinging aphrodisiac sauce – I tell you, I could hardly waddle home, or compose my sentiments. So Clive gets a little warm & very red about the gills towards midnight.

Then Karin, who felt the approach of disillusionment about eleven, ran down to the kitchen & borrowed the housemaids' gramophone. The 40 young men began waltzing, & the three lovely girls sat together flirting in corners. Isn't it an odd thing that Bloomsbury parties are always thus composed – 40 young men; all from Oxford too, & three girls, who are admitted on condition that they either dress exquisitely, or are some man's mistress, or love each other. Much preferring my own sex as I do, or at any rate, finding the monotony of young men's conversation considerable, & resenting the eternal pressure which they put, if you're a woman, on one string, find the disproportion excessive, & intend to cultivate women's society entirely in future. Men are all in the light always: with women you swim at once into the silent dusk. But to return. They danced. Leonard got horribly bored. He was set upon by little Eddie Sackville-West, who is as appealing as a kitten, a stray, a mangy, unloved kitten; & this poor boy, after pouring forth his woes (all men confide in Leonard – especially such as love their own sex) sat by mistake down on the best tea cups. Being an aristocrat out of his element, he was considerably discomposed. Sweets & jams, stuck to his behind. And Leonard had to dust him, & pat him, & finally leave him; trying I believe, to smoke a pipe in full evening dress & white waistcoat. They work very hard, the aristocracy. Karin was heard to say, between the waltzes, Isn't this Jolly? – On being assured it was, she plucked up heart, & means to give another party, with another hostess, next month.

Really, you have done me good, This is the first time I have cantered out on paper this fortnight. I find a great pleasure in waking all the doves in their dovecots – in stirring my words again. But this I can never explain to a painter, I suppose: how words live in companies, never used, except when one writes.

What about the autobiography? You jeered at me for saying I would print it. But I swear I will. I can see the very book it shall be, & if you don't look out, I shall add to it some of your pictures, with a description of them from my own pen. (this is a threat, because writers can't write about anything except writing)

So now I must stop, & do a little cross stitch, & I shall dwell upon you, as indeed I have been doing a great deal, lying here – & though you'll snap my nose off for saying so – with admiration as well as affection.

Yrs

VW

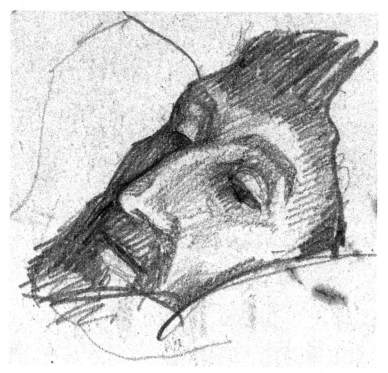

Jacques ill in bed, by Gwen Raverat, pencil

This is the last letter from Jacques to Virginia. It was accompanied by Gwen's letter announcing his death (page 158).

dictated to Gwen Raverat   February 1925

My dear Virginia,

I am writing to you now, first because I like it, & then because it's less trouble than trying to remember what happened 15 or 20 years ago. It all seems on looking back so infinitely complex, & it's so difficult to sort out the threads. I am quite as morbid as you can be about my work & I don't know that I shall let you see what I've written. Its much too crude & simple & absurdly romantic too. But then I suppose I was romantic in those days. I was interested in Roger's appreciation of my pictures. Of course I like praise; & a few years ago a little encouragement would have helped me & meant a great deal to me. I suppose I had to find my own way in pride & isolation, but believe me, it wasn't because I shouldn't have liked success; & I think I wasted a great deal of time. I should like Roger (& you) to see my latest work. It's 100% better than anything he can have seen. I ought to have 20 or 30 years work ahead of me, & instead of that, now …

I am glad the flowers pleased you, but its a little early yet, & I wish you could see the wild flowers in April & May & June up in the hills.

Of course you're right to write for *Vogue*, if they pay you enough, especially if that American thinks it 'demeaning'. But you wouldn't expect him to know the meaning

Jacques Raverat, by Gwen Raverat,
wood engraving (actual size), 1925

of ordinary English words. They are all prigs & humbugs, & their minds are childish.

Sodomy: perfectly natural & normal up to the age of about 20. After that, I don't know why, faintly disgusting to me. It seems to me a state of arrested development, of people who don't ever quite grow up. It's also rather ridiculous. Perhaps you've heard that Gide has written a dull little, dreary little book in defence of it, called *Corydon*. I suggested that it was both useless & absurd to make excuses & that anyhow Proust had said more than enough on the subject. 'Ah,' he answered, 'but Proust has left out all the really fine & noble side of it.' And finally it gets excessively boring when they will talk of nothing else. Sapphism seems to me much more attractive & understandable, with all those surplus, unattached women about. They must find, shall we say, some outlet for their passions, poor things.

I am most eagerly looking forward to your novel & I *do* appreciate the honour & the exception, more than I can tell you. I can't read much to myself now, but I can still listen, & my mind feels clearer & more lucid than ever.

I still think of what you said in a former letter about the impression you had of me & Gwen all those years ago. How little we do understand about one another, & is it really impossible to know the truth? I remember so well that evening when I made you smoke a cigar. You wanted to be admired, & I *was* all admiration, full of diffidence, feeling infinitely young & wishing I were a little more grown-up. I can't help thinking we should understand one another better now. Experience does help in that at least, though it usually comes

151

too late like everything else. But I wish I could make my own view of myself & my life agree with what other people seem to think. It would be so much comfortabler. I liked getting the photograph of Leonard (I remember you said once I was not to call him Woolf.) He's changed I think much less than you have, & is just as I remember him. I'd like to paint him. (N.B. I don't mean to imply that you have changed for the worse – au contraire.)

We are having a visit from Eily. I know you prefer Bernard – a mere Darwin – but I love Eily very much. She is wise & mellow & humourous & tolerant, & she has warmth of heart & a lightness of touch, unsurpassed, which are very endearing qualities. Perhaps she's not very clever, but then there are such a lot of clever people, that it doesn't seem to me so important as it used.

We talked about you a great deal, as you can guess, & we agreed on one point, that you were probably, of all the people that we both knew, the happiest. But how can one tell about a person one hasn't seen for so many years. I wonder if it's true; & I wonder if you think it's true. It's, in my mind, a great compliment, let me tell you. I think *I* should have had a certain gift for happiness also; but destiny or fate or whatever you call it has broken me to bits instead. An awful waste.

Goodbye dear Virginia

Jacques

P. S. Feb 9th

I wrote this at intervals during the last fortnight & was just going to send it off; & now your letter has come &

your book. Almost it's enough to make me want to live a little longer, to continue to receive such letters & such books. I don't know how to thank you. I am flattered (& *you* know how important an element that is in one's sensations) & proud & pleased & we've already read the first 40 pages of *Mrs Dalloway*. How tiresome that we can't talk. I should so love you to be autobiographical & egotistical & indiscreet. But then surely it's the morbid influence of your distemper that makes you think so, that you don't live because you are a writer. I cannot believe that you or I have *Anything* to learn from, say, Clive Bell, about living; thought or feeling or sensation, eating or loving. I cannot believe that he is really 'red hot' but in your imagination. It's true I didn't like either his appearance or his manners, but I dare say he has a kind heart. Everybody says so. Probably I am quite wrong & anyhow it doesn't matter much. I wonder how you would like the exclusive company of women. Not for long, I suspect. One wants a change. Certainly your description of Leonard's account of Karin's party would rather cool my curiosity to see life in Bloomsbury again. It sounds infinitely tedious. But *I* should have talked to you. And our wit would have made those pallid painted young creatures gasp. I've been trying to write, not my autobiography any more, it bores me, but the history of Rupert. It's much better, I think, but I advance with prodigious slowness. It all seems so vain & hopeless, as I feel sure I shall not have the time or the strength to finish it. I think I understand partly what you say about using words. They & colours become like ghosts & recede, if you don't go on

Vence, La Place en Hiver, by Gwen Raverat,
wood engraving (reduced in size), 1923

using them – writing or painting I mean. This is a long
letter; I'm afraid you'll find it rather a gloomy & melancholy one; but I can't help it, & I'll do you the honour of
not making pretences. You ought to come out here to re-
cover from your influenza; the weather is constant sun-
shine. I send you my thanks again & my best love.

  Jacques

dictated to Gwen Raverat
Villa Adèle   9th February 1925

My dearest [Gwen],
    I know I love you and I think you love me. Anyhow your love has been the best thing in my life. I send you this for you to keep and remember if you get morbid.

I love you, Jacques.

Don't spoil Elisabeth.
Be happy and make her happy.
Keep well and remember to varnish my pictures.

Jacques had eaten nothing but spoonfuls of Bengers Food and some sugar for the last two months. He slept peacefully until the last four days when he suddenly found it difficult to talk and to swallow. Jean Marchand was by Gwen's side throughout.

Villa Adèle   [early March 1925]

  He sleeps nearly all day long, he is very near the end; he can't see plain. But he's pretty comfortable mostly – with a good deal of morphine – And when he's awake he talks and talks and talks; for hours at a time; making plans for my future, journeys I'm to go on, things I'm to paint. – I stick tight to the knowledge that it's best so. The last two years were I suppose just worth it, but only just; only because he was painting better and better; the rest of his life was hell. Since October it's not been good enough.

FROM GWEN RAVERAT TO MARGARET KEYNES

Villa Adèle   [March 1925]

… I couldn't have got through it without Marchand, though of course he couldn't do anything but hang about … The doctor wouldn't come till I made him, and then wouldn't look or help and got away as quick as he could. He was frightened and upset I think, but I do think he might have been more use.

The drawings opposite were made by Gwen of Jacques on his death bed on 7th March. 'The shock of those last four days and the last hours especially was dreadful. It was a mad horrible incredible nightmare. I try to forget but I can't,' she wrote to Margaret 12 days later. The letter she refers to is the long one that starts on page149.

8th March 1925

Dear Virginia,

Jacques died last night. This letter was all written by bits till he was too weak to write any more. He told me to send it with his love. I think your letters were one of the greatest pleasures of these last weeks, perhaps the greatest. I do thank you for them and *Mrs Dalloway*. I shan't try to tell you what I think of *her* – it's much the same as what Jacques thinks; in fact I really believe several of his remarks were cribbed from me.

It's impossible to me to write decently about all this last time. I wish you would write to me. I do thank you again dearest Virginia

Gwen

52 Tavistock Square   11th March [1925]

Dearest Gwen,

Your & Jacques' letter came yesterday, & I go about think-ing of you both, in starts, & almost constantly underneath everything, & I don't know what to say. One thing that comes over & over is the strange wish I have to go on telling Jacques things. This is for Jacques, I say to myself; I want to write to him about happiness, & about Rupert, & love. It had be-come to me a sort of private life, & I believe I told him more than anyone, except Leonard: I become mystical as I grow older & feel an alliance with you & Jacques which is eternal, not interrupted, or hurt by never meeting. Then, of course, I have now for you – how can I put it? – I mean the feeling that one must reverence? – is that the word – feel shy of, so tremendous an experience; for I cannot conceive what you have suffered. It seems to me that if we met, one would have to chatter about every sort of little trifle, because there is nothing to be said.

And then, being, as you know, so fundamentally an opti-mist, I want to make you enjoy life. Forgive me, for writ-ing what comes into my head. I think I feel that I would give a great deal to share with you the daily happinesses. But you know that if there is anything I could ever give you, I would give it, but perhaps the only thing to give is to be oneself with people. One could say anything to Jacques. And that will always be the same with you & me. But oh, dearest

52 Tavistock Sqre.

11th March.

Dearest Gwen,

Your & Jacques' letter came yesterday, & I go about thinking of you both, in starts, & almost constantly underneath everything, & I don't know what to say. The thing that comes over & over is the strange wish I have to go on telling Jacques things. This is for Jacques, I say to myself; I want to write to him about happiness, & about Rupert, & love. What become to me a sort of private life, & I believe I told him more than anyone, except Leonard: I become mystical as I grow older & feel an alliance with you & Jacques which is eternal, not interrupted, or hurt by never meeting. Then, ploure, I have now for you a — how can I put it? — I mean the feeling that one must reverence? — is that the word — feel shy of, so tremendous an experience; for I cannot conceive what you have suffered. It seems to me that if we met, one would have to chatter about every sort of little thing, because there is nothing to be said. And then, being, as you know, so fundamentally an optimist, I want to make you enjoy life. Forgive me, for writing on what comes into my head. I think I feel that I would give a great deal to share with you the daily happinesses. But you know that if there is anything I could ever give you, I would give it, but perhaps the only thing to give is to be oneself with people. One could say anything

Gwen, to think of you is making me cry – Why should you & Jacques have had to go through this? As I told him, it is your love that has forever been love to me – all those years ago, when you used to come to Fitzroy Square, & I was so angry: & you were so furious, & Jacques wrote me a sensible manly letter, which I answered, sitting at my table in the window. Perhaps I was frightfully jealous of you both, being at war with the whole world at the moment. Still, the vision has become to me a source of wonder – the vision of your face; which, if I were painting, I should cover with flames & put you on a hill top. Then, I don't think you would believe how it moves me that you & Jacques should have been reading *Mrs Dalloway*, & liking it [*JR did not express an opinion in his previous letter – just that they had read 40 pages. GR's later remark that 'Jacques said all I wanted to' about* Mrs Dalloway, *along with VW's subsequent reference to such a letter, suggests JR wrote another which is now lost.*]. I'm awfully vain I know; & I was on pins & needles about sending it to Jacques; & now I feel exquisitely relieved; not flattered; but one does want that side of one to be acceptable – I was going to have written to Jacques about his children, & about my having none – I mean, these efforts of mine to communicate with people are partly childlessness, & the horror that sometimes overcomes me.

There's very little use in writing this. One feels so ignorant, so trivial, & like a child, just teasing you. But it is only that one keeps thinking of you, with a sort of reverence, & of that adorable man, whom I loved.

Yrs V. W.

Villa Adèle,
Vence, A.M.   Sunday March 15 1925

My dearest Virginia,

Your letter moved me very much. I think you know that I always did love you & trust you. Isn't it odd, do you know I'd completely forgotten that time when I was so angry & you too – till Jacques talked of it lately.

But you know, really, the worst is over now. I think I am going to be happy in a quiet sort of way. The worst was over long ago I think – or perhaps about two years ago was the worst of all. The day I gave all his boots away & knew he would never walk again – ages ago – there ought to have been a hearse & undertakers to take them away, but no one knew of course. But now – Virginia – I think I am like one of those spiders that eat up their husbands when they have done with them; I've eaten up Jacques, & there he is inside me for as long as I live. I'm not even lonely so far, I have had him so entirely. I suppose I shall be some-times, but not very much. It's the things you *haven't* had that hurt most; or perhaps they don't hurt most exactly, but they are worse to bear. Like your childlessness. I think I know about that & how it makes you feel cut off from everything & everybody – But you aren't really you know. For instance no one else but you has got so near to me now – no one else except Marchand who loved Jacques & whom Jacques loved, & who has been right through the horrors of these last months with us. Because they have been terrible – I don't use that word lightly – & the last few days were a mad nightmare I wish I could forget.

Virginia, when we're very old, sixty or so, I'd like to tell you the whole history of my life, as truly as I could; it seems to me it has been so strange; perhaps not stranger than others? I don't know. No, I do feel sure that some of it isn't ordinary – And you must tell me yours, if you will. For I have always wanted to know what was happening to you in those years in Fitzroy Square. I used dimly to perceive things, but was too shy & discreet to ask, & so I never knew.

I think, you know, that you idealize us – Jacques & me; at least I'm afraid of it & that when you see me again you'll see its deal and not oak at all I'm made of. I wish you could see the pictures Jacques did in the last year, or 2 years. He was very slow in starting, I think; very slow in getting really under way, perhaps because it was so much his own & not other people's. But there aren't enough of these last things – not enough, not enough – I suppose it's all lost. Everything lost, except the bit I've got inside me, & the bits other people may have picked up.

I wonder if I'm being sentimental. I don't much care if I am, its nearer the truth than *not* being sentimental I think. But I think, in spite of everything, Jacques was happy really; happier than most people; till just these last few months, & even then, when living was almost impossible, it seemed even more impossible for him to die.

But Virginia, the thing that hurt really & that nobody knows or guesses, is the thought of the times I hurt him, so much, in these last years. I know it was inevitable & human; it was only that I was alive & couldn't help wanting to live, & that he was dying & partly dead – the slow tearing apart of us – I hurt him infernally. But we got through it, anyhow, somehow; it was all right; *Don't tell all that please*.

But now you see, the daily happinesses are just what I *can* have; just what I've not been able to have for years, just what it hurt Jacques so to feel me wanting. I do think I'm going to be happy. It's all over you see, the suffering is over. It so happened that we read *Anthony & Cleopatra* last of all.

I can't write like you & I'm absurdly afraid of saying things that set one's teeth on edge (as Will Arnold Forster does for instance.) Please will you tell me if this that I've written is indecent or sentimental; I really don't know & I want to. There are some things in life, that some of us know about, but that it is indecent to write about – some kinds of pain I think. Do you agree? We've just got to pretend it isn't so, or life can't go on at all.

Like the Goya etchings, & some parts of Shakespeare. Nobody takes any notice of them or of what they mean because they daren't I suppose. Nor the Christians: they miss altogether the final cry of Christ 'My God, my God why hast thou forsaken me?' which denies all the rest; I've never heard any Christian comment on it, they skip it. (I'm not a Christian at all – don't be afraid.) – That is to say most people have to pretend it isn't so – but people who've been through it don't & can't – (like you, who've been mad) only one has to be awfully careful how one writes or talks about it. This is all getting too muddled – I shall stop.

Now to be practical. I suppose you & Leonard couldn't come & stay with me any time this spring. I can't tell you how I should like it. I'm going to Italy – (a queer party – me, Marchand & my brother Charles – however we seem to get on very well –) for a week or so, starting in a few days' time; but after that I've no plans. Later some time I'm going to Paris to hunt for a flat or a house, either there or at Versailles or St Germain or somewhere. I shall hope to move away from here in the autumn. And I should like you to see the beauty of this place – before its quite spoilt by the English.

Ka, in a woolly headed letter, said you'd been ill since you had influenza. Wouldn't it be good for you to come? I've got a car, I can drive, so can Babette. We might have great fun. I shall paint you. Babette will make good strong French jokes – country ones, not Paris ones. Perhaps la Pozzi & Valéry will be here, or Marchand not gone yet. (But I can't promise any of those people) Still I think it might be fun. And I should so love it. Come soon, if you possibly can. – I feel as if I want to thank you again & again for writing to Jacques & sending *Mrs Dalloway*. I've not said any more about her, because really Jacques said all I wanted to; but I keep thinking about it & the splendour of the day & the sort of *ballet* of life you give. I think it is a wonderful thing to have done.

Dear Virginia, you must keep on loving me because I do want it so much & I am so glad you loved Jacques.

GR.

52 Tavistock Square, WC   Sunday, March 22nd [1925]

Dearest Gwen,

It was a great relief to get your letter. I had been feeling that perhaps I had said something idiotically foolish, to hurt you more. Not that one is hurt by foolish things however. But this is a practical letter – We are going on the 26th to Hotel Cendrillon Cassis [*just to the West of Marseilles*] for 10 days. That is all the time we can get off, owing to our books; but if you could come & stay a night, do. I'm afraid you will be in Italy then. I don't see any chance of going abroad later – we have a new man come to work, & he is anxious about being left alone. But write later, & suggest meeting somehow else.

Yes, I will tell you the whole of my life history one day, but I think it was my affair with Clive & Nessa I was think-ing of when I said I envied you & Jacques at Fitzroy Square [*The affair Virginia refers to was with Clive Bell in 1909*]. For some reason that turned more of a knife in me than any-thing else has ever done.

What about the thing Jacques was writing? Can I see it? Also, have you a snapshot or any photograph of him?

I go on making things up to tell him; & shall have to go on writing to you I believe.

But not now. Molly MacCarthy has been in, like a dream-ing moth, to give me a copy of Shakespeare, & now we have to dine with Clive: I'm quite well again, but had to put my head under my wing & sleep for a month.

Write if you would ever care to; for I should like nothing better.

Yrs

VW

We shall be at Cassis till Monday 6th.

The Princess Lost,
by Gwen Raverat,
wood engraving
(actual size), 1926

52 Tavistock Square   April 8th 1925

Dearest Gwen,

   After all we had to come back a day earlier than we meant,
as the hotel became crowded. But we had snuffed up every
moment – it was fine incessantly, & I now see why you &
Jacques pitched on the borders of that sea. But I was going, inconsistently, to beg you to live in London. Trust me
to find you a house. Then I would flirt with your daughters, & talk the sun out of the sky with you. Paris is a hos-
tile brilliant alien city. Nancy Cunard & Hope Mirrlees &
myriads of the ineffective English live there, or rather hop
from rock to rock. Here we grow slowly & sedately in our
own soil. Coming back last night was like stepping into
some grave twilit room, very spacious & quiet, with a few
lights & the great misty squares, & everything very mute,
& snuffled, & out at elbows.

   I cannot think what I was going to write to Jacques about
love. I constantly thought of him at Cassis. I thought of
him lying among those terraces & vineyards, where it is all
so clearest, & logical & intense; & it struck me that, from
not having seen him all these years, I have no difficulty in
thinking him still alive. That is what I should like for myself; that there should be no breach, no submission to death,
but merely a break in the talk. I liked that uncompromis-
ing reality of his: no sentimentality, & no beating about

the bush. This is all very ill written, chopped & jerky, when I should like to write even the racketiest letter to Gwen beautifully, but I went out early this morning to see Nessa's new house [*37 Gordon Square*], & saw a woman killed by a motor car – This pitches one at once into a region where there is no certainty, & one feels somehow, abject & cowed & exalted. I want so much to understand my own feelings about everything; to unravel, & re-christen, & not go dreaming my time away. Jacques' death will probably make you, because it will so intensify everything, a very interesting woman to me. But as I said before, I cannot conceive such an experience; not at your age.

I feel that Jacques was thinking a great deal of Rupert at the end. Rupert was a little mythical to me when he died. He was very rude to Nessa once; & Leonard, I think, rather disliked him; in fact Bloomsbury was against him, & he against them. Meanwhile, I had a private version of him which I stuck to when they all cried him down, & still preserve somewhere infinitely far away – but how these feelings last, how they come over one, oddly, at un-expected moments – based on my week at Grantchester [*in 1911*], when he was all that could be kind & interesting & substantial & downhearted (I choose these words without thinking whether they correspond to what he was to you or anybody). He was, I thought, the ablest of all the young men; I did not then think much of his poetry, which he read aloud on the lawn; but I thought he would be Prime Minister, because he had such a gift with people, & such sanity, & force; I remember a weakly pair of lovers, meandering in one day, just engaged, & very floppy (A.Y. Campbell & his bride who now writes on Shelley). You know how intense & silly & offhand in a self-conscious kind of way the Cambridge young then were about their loves – Rupert simplified them, & broadened them, – humanised them – And then he rode off on a bicycle about a railway strike. Jacques says he thinks Rupert's poetry was poetry. I must read it again. I had come to think it mere barrel organ music, but this refers to the patriotic poems, & perhaps is unfair: but the early ones were all adjectives & contortions, weren't they? My idea was that he was to be member of Parliament, & edit the classics: a very powerful, ambitious man, but not a poet. Still all this is no doubt wholly & completely wrong.

This morning, to hearten myself, I read Jacques letter about *Mrs Dalloway* again. I was afraid, & indeed half sure, he wouldn't like it, or I meant to have asked him to let me dedicate it to him. When you have time one day, do tell me why you liked it – or anything about it. This is partly author's vanity & that consuming interest in one's own work which is not entirely vanity – & partly it springs from my own feeling that to be brought before you & Jacques was a tremendous ordeal, at that time, & the impression it made on you would mean more to me than what other people could say of it. But forgive this importunity. I am off for Easter to Rodmell – a place you'll have to visit. But when are you coming over? I can't tell you how that 10 days at Cassis has burnt itself upon my mind's eye – the beauty, & our happiness, & you & Jacques. Well – I am interrupted by an author, who rings up & says he or she must deliver a manuscript into my own hands. What about Jacques' autobiography?

This is a scrap but only in meaning, for it is too long, but I am too harried to write a nice letter, & yet I don't think you mind whether one writes a nice letter or not, so I shall send it. And I will certainly keep up the habit of garrulity, to which Jacques induced me. I never write a word to anybody nowadays – except for him, I don't think I wrote a letter in 8 weeks.

Tell me about your children.

Does the little creature write more poems?

Yrs VW

Wednesday, 8th April 1925

Since I wrote, which is these last months, Jacques Raverat has died; after longing to die; and he sent me a letter about *Mrs Dalloway* which gave me one of the happiest days of my life. I wonder if this time I have achieved something? Well, nothing anyhow compared with Proust, in whom I am embedded now. The thing about Proust is his combination of the utmost sensibility with the utmost tenacity. He searches out these butterfly shades to the last grain. He is as tough as catgut & as evanescent as a butterfly's bloom. And he will I suppose both influence me and make me out of temper with every sentence of my own. Jacques died, as I say; and at once the siege of emotions began. I got the news with a party here – Clive, Bee How, Julia Strachey, Dadie. Nevertheless, I do not any longer feel inclined to doff the cap to death. I like to go out of the room talking, with an unfinished casual sentence on my lips. That is the effect it had on me – no leavetakings, no submission – but someone stepping out into the darkness. For her though the nightmare was terrific. All I can do now is to keep natural with her, which is I believe a matter of considerable importance. More & more do I repeat my own version of Montaigne 'Its life that matters'.

Babette, the Raverats' faithful nanny, had fallen in love with Gwen's younger brother Billy when he was in Vence and became pregnant by him. They got engaged, but she died in the operating theatre from a strangulated hernia when in Ireland that August. Meanwhile Gwen had fallen in love with Jean Marchand. Soon she left Vence for good and spent time in Paris, while the children were sent to their Barlow cousins who lived in Chesham Bois and holidayed in Norfolk.

Villa Adèle,
Vence, AM   22nd April 1925

My dear Virginia,

   I've just finished reading *Mrs Dalloway* again. I *do* think it damn good. I feel horribly jealous of you. You're only 3 years older than me, and you've done that. You say I'm to write about it – well, I like it because it's all of a piece. *Jacob*, I liked, but to my mind it didn't come together into a whole. Perhaps it was too long. But *Mrs Dalloway* is such a very good composition (in the painting sense). I like the way it works up to the end. The end is splendid. And the people are all alive. I didn't think they always were in your earlier books. But now the whole thing is alive and moving; it's like a ballet. That's what you meant, isn't it? All the movements in different directions both in time and in space, going on at the same time. But here is, not a criticism, but a question: there was one bit I had to skip when I read it to Jacques – about Septimus – pages 102 & 138. It was too dreadful. It is all right afterwards, one doesn't mind any of the rest of the mad parts. And I think it may have been that in our state of mind just then we couldn't stand any more horrors; not that it is really too horrible. I don't mean it isn't true, only can one say it with decency – ? I wish you would write a book about decency. I'm sure there *is* such a thing, it isn't squeamishness, it is that certain things – horrors or intimacies or heroisms or madness – have to be written about with very great restraint else they get out of key. Is it that? Tell me what you think? Or do you think one can say anything about anything? I think one probably can if it's said in the right way; but the right way must be very hard to find sometime – But all this is abstract. I don't really know if that bit of madness in *Mrs D.* is worse than any of the rest, or if it only coincided to us with a realization of the madness in which we were living ourselves; and now it's got coloured by our situation and I shall never get it free again and be able to judge it clearly.

I'm going to send you a photograph of a painting I did of Jacques when I've had it photographed. There are no decent photographs of him, and the painting, whatever its other merits, is like him. About his M.S. – I'm going to get it typewritten and then see how it looks. He told me to burn it, and not to show it anyone, much less you. Does one obey the dead? I think one judges oneself. It couldn't ever be published anyhow, because it would hurt his father's feelings dreadfully. I *think* I shall send it to you – it is so very like Jacques. It's only his 3 years at Bedales. The rest is too much unfinished. I've also got for you a little sketch of

175

his – a figure – But he was very humble about that, and said I was to see if you liked it and *on no account whatsoever* to give it to you unless you really did. That will be when I come to England.

You've missed one point about Rupert: that he didn't really care about life. He was ambitious but he didn't love things for themselves. All that about bathing and food and bodies was a pose. He didn't care – not like Jacques. And when a fly bit him, he just died out of carelessness. And so I wouldn't call him substantial, as you do, unless you mean the schoolmaster side of him – the responsible practical fatherly man. He *was* a schoolmaster. For instance, he tried so hard to prevent all the friends whom he considered young and innocent from being enticed into your bawdy houses at Bloomsbury. Of course Bloomsbury disliked him; how could they help it, when he thought them so infinitely corrupt and sinister that no one (except himself) could be trusted to enter their purlieus and come out unsmirched. I don't quite know why he thought Bloomsbury so devilishly poisonous, but he did – (and was it perhaps true that they weren't very good for the-not-very-strong-in-the-head such as Margery Olivier? or the vain and credulous and cotton wool-stuffed such as Ka? What do you think? Oughtn't women like that to go to church and be kept at their father's coat tails until they are married and safe? Or doesn't it matter either way?)

But Jacques wouldn't have gone and died like Rupert. He, more than anyone I've ever known, did care about things and about living. Right up to the very end – to within a

by Gwen Raverat, wood engraving (actual size), 1919

week of his death, he didn't *really* want to die: though he said he did; or really quite believe that he was going to die, in spite of all the horrors he went through. It's that that makes it seem so incredible that he's dead. He lay there planning our journeys – journeys for me to go – journeys for Marchand – places I was to take Elisabeth to – dinners to eat (when the thought of food made him feel sick). No one but he could have lived so long in that state. And though he had lost nearly all possible physical pleasures, yet he could somehow taste the memory of them in his impotence with more force than Rupert ever could their reality in all his youth.

And yet, somehow life has seemed duller ever since Rupert died. And now it's much duller still. I don't mean the substance of things isn't as strange as ever; only there's no one to talk to about it. I suppose because I find it hard to get things into Language. *You*, a writer can talk to me, and (I think) I understand – but can I talk to you; do you understand? the things I care about are so dumb.

I've begun painting again and am simply bogged and bewildered and lost – and where I ought to have been 12 years ago. I wonder if I shall get clear ever.

I'm going to try life in Paris rather in a spirit of adventure, with a feeling I can pull back on London, if I don't like it in a year or two. But I like living in France; I feel always free-er and more myself and I don't ever have to pretend to be an English lady and really very nice. (I suppose perhaps I am all that really. No, damn it I'm not) And Jacques wanted the children to be French; I think Elisabeth is very French and will be happier in France; and Sophie will be happy and successful anywhere I believe, because she knows how to manage life – when to put head-foremost and when to slide round sideways. Now Elisabeth never knows. She is Jacques' daughter, in spirit especially, though she's not at all clever or brilliant. But she has his touch, his sense of beauty and colour, his lack of responsibility – and his richness of nature ... I can't explain. Here are some more poems – but don't read them unless they amuse you, and burn them. Jacques thought her use of words very good indeed, but he was probably partial. She is very young and unsophisticated, and not at all like Janey Bussy. Reads only fairy tales and thinks all day about Princesses, la sainte Vierge, fairies, brigands, etc.

What a letter – do write again –

Yours ever,

Gwen.

Jean Marchand, by Gwen Raverat, pencil, 1925

On 4th May she went with Leonard to Cambridge, where he was to attend an Apostles' meeting. She wrote in her diary how, on her way to dinner at Newnham College, 'walking past the Darwins [at Newnham Grange] *I noticed the willows; I thought with that growing maternal affection which now comes to me, of myself there; of Rupert.'*

52 Tavistock Square   1st May [1925]

My dear Gwen,

   It comes into my head to write to you, because I ought to be doing so many other things, & have refused to go to the Private view of the Royal Academy to do them; & now sit down & write to you, instead. I wish you didn't feel dumb: but, I reflect, you're a square-tipped painter; (& painters' fingers are square); & I always connect this with some impermeability. You all live in the depths of the sea; except indeed Jacques, who was half chatterbox, as I am wholly chatterbox. Even now, I've so much to say to you, I can't begin. I wish you had someone to talk to. I wish I could be in reach of you. I believe somehow we should set up communication. You should paint, & I should walk about talking. Now & again you would take the brush from your lips & make some sagacious remark. That is the devil of these deaths – Thoby's & Jacques: they leave life duller; & that is what one resents [*Thoby died of typhoid in 1906, aged 26*]. Not the horror of the moment; but the flatness afterwards. But don't let it – let us polish off that demon. Indeed, my respect & belief in you is such that I can believe you will be a superb character, after my own heart. For, to tell you the truth, I have so little faith in myself, that I glorify some of my friends. Then you're younger than I am; & I feel bidden to stand in the relation to you of elder & wiser. Did you ever think of that? Do you remember an evening at the Grange, & the poplar trees, & Margaret talking about Pragmatism? It comes back to me, half visually, the lawn & the poplars. What you say about *Mrs Dalloway* is exactly what I was after. I had a sort of terror that I had inflicted something on you, sending you that book at that moment. I will look at the scenes you mention. It was a subject that I have kept cooling in my mind until I felt I could touch it without bursting into flame all over. You can't think what a raging furnace it is still to me – madness & doctors & being forced. But lets change the subject.

Let me have anything you will of Jacques'. I miss him so queerly. It is that obstinate life of his that would never be submissive that I find myself wanting; his hard, truculent mind. And reading his letters again I find he says I knew very little of him really. Tell me more one of these days. I like making him up as I walk about London – now to buy a cup of coffee, now to take tea with Lady Colefax, who interests me, as you would be interested by a shiny cupboard carved with acanthus leaves, to hold whisky – so hard & shiny & bright is she; & collects all the intellects about her, as a parrot picks up beads, without knowing Lord Balfour from Duncan Grant. Now I want to discuss your view, or Rupert's view of Bloomsbury but have no time.

After all, I always wind up, if six people, with no special start except what their wits give them, can so dominate, there must be some reason in it. And what Rupert never allowed for was that half of them were every bit as lacerated & sceptical & unhappy as he was. Where they seem to me to triumph is in having worked out a view of life which was not by any means corrupt or sinister or merely intellectual; rather ascetic & austere indeed; which still holds, & keeps them dining together, & staying together, after 20 years; & no amount of quarrelling or success, or failure has altered this. Now I do think this rather creditable. But tell me, who *is* Bloomsbury in your mind? Tell me too what you are painting. I like the poems – but how is she being taught? Does she read? They are like a child singing – very pure & lovely.

Is Ka vain? And what is Eily like? Eily is on my conscience at the moment.

I am going to Cambridge this weekend, & will write to you – tell you what odds & ends I pick up. And do believe that I wish to understand you ; I know, one can't; but it is a genuine thing in my life – your going on alone.

And you must forgive me for all sorts of follies in my letters , my dear Gwen.

VW

On Elisabeth Singing
for JR

by Frances Cornford

You who, frustrated, died so long ago
In night and pain, but left a child to grow
Passionate spirit, in the shades rejoice
All that you suffered and knew is in her voice.

Friday, 27th November 1925

Gwen comes in: threatens to dissolve, her hearty direct stodgy manner in floods of tears, as if the rivets that hold her must give way – such tragedies have beaten her, together for the moment; but suddenly she will break down & tell me something that she has not told anyone. She finds me understanding. And I suppose she is in love – or Marchand in love – & I don't altogether want to hear it.

Tuesday, 23rd February 1926

Here is the usual door bell/ & I think Gwen came in, & I was rather sodden & wretched, feeling that I had nothing to give her, & she everything to ask. As I foretold, she is enmeshed in a net of fire: that is the truth; loves net; the fiery net of – who was it? – that was scorched to death: & hers is more painful than his, & more enduring. Yet how seldom one envisages what one knows! Her net lies on me; but it does not burn me. And I do little futile kindnesses to her, which are little good to anybody; & I don't do them, & I feel compunction.

England 1928 to 1953

GWEN MOVES BACK TO CAMBRIDGE

After living in Bloomsbury, contributing wood engravings, draw-
ings and art criticism for Time & Tide *magazine and develop-*
ing her career as a book illustrator, Gwen moved from London to
Harlton, near Cambridge in 1929. In 1940 she acted on her con-
victions about the war effort and went to work in her Uncle
Horace's company, the Cambridge Instrument Company, check-
ing thermometers for aeroplanes. But she soon got bored with
this and went to work for the Admiralty, who had taken over the
Scott Polar Research Institute, making perspective line drawings
of ordnance survey maps of the Pacific Islands. In August 1942,
to be nearer her work and with both her daughters married, she
moved to Conduit Head Road in Cambridge as a near neighbour
of her Cornford cousins. In the spring of 1946 she moved into
the Old Granary in Silver Street.

In the same period Virginia Woolf published some of her great-
est work and acheived a worldwide reputation. She took her
life on March 28th, 1941, writing in her note to Leonard, 'I
know I shall never get over this: & I am wasting your life. It is
this madness.'

FROM GWEN RAVERAT TO VIRGINIA WOOLF

On her return to London, Gwen's depression was helped by her move to Mecklenburgh Square where 'Old Bloomsbury' gave her some support, though Virginia was slow to understand the fragility of Gwen's mental condition. Sophie went to school with Vanessa Bell's daughter Angelica, while Elisabeth went to the school Marjorie Strachey had set up at Charleston for one term. Gwen's 'halfcaste' was Gerald Meade to whom she sublet her first-floor rooms.

5 Caroline Place,
Mecklenburgh Square, WC1   Tuesday. [1928?]

Dear Virginia

I'm so sorry I forgot before to write: my young halfcaste French and Englishman is going to Siam for a permanent job; so he is no use (I did write to him). I can't think of any one else at the moment.

I meant to write before to say it was nice of you to send me that note the other day: you are never dull, as you know perfectly well. Nothing is duller than a continuous sparkle, or so I think. (And then you are beautiful.) I know you like that said – it's very bad for your morals that it's so true.

What I really wanted to say (and the reason I didn't write before is that its so difficult to express) – is that being unhappy is to my mind both so boring and so disgusting, that I feel I would like to apologize to the world for being so, or only it were not so ridiculous to do it. I am getting very much saner now. I can *read* again, it is so lovely after

2½ years of not being able to read a word. – What I am trying to say is that I think you understand enough for me not to mind having let you be a part of how mad I was .... don't you?

Anyhow, I don't really care, only it must have been rather horrid (and dull) for you.

Yes, I *am* better. I don't like being mad at all.

Yrs ever, Gwen.

P.S. I like Leonard.

Fontcreuse,
Cassis,
B. du R.,
France   7th April [1928]

My Dear Gwen,

I wish I could have gone to see your pictures, but we left England the day after the show began [*GR's exhibition at the St George's Gallery, 23rd March to 12th April*], & I suppose it will be over when we come back – about the 20th. I should have liked to see them, not from artistic reasons, but to make up my idea of your character. I have no illusions about my artistic criticism. It is all literary. Were you pleased with the show? I have a kind of idea that we may meet one day this summer. It is an almost impossible achievement. Human beings are so terrified of each other. If I rang your bell I should feel certain you did not want to see me, as I walked up stairs – I should feel I am committing an intrusion. All the same, I think I shall.

We motored from Dieppe to Cassis – absolute heaven, I think it. Everything looks odd & new, coming along the road to it gradually. I'm half inclined to buy a barn here in a vineyard. The sun & the hills put my dear London rather in the shade – & then one does exactly what one likes here.

What are you up to?

Yrs

VW

In 1927 Virginia introduced Gwen to Lady Rhondda, founder and editor of the magazine Time and Tide, *and Gwen continued to provide drawings and wood engravings to the magazine for many years. In 1929 Gwen started to write art criticism and book reviews for the magazine.*

THE LONDON GROUP
by Gwendolen Raverat

The London Group represents a certain school of painting, and has become almost as academic as the Academy, in its way. It is the fate of groups. Just as the New English Art Club rose, flourished, declined and now lingers on in an anaemic way; so the London Group rose and flourished and has begun to decline; and so will she live on in her own turgid manner, long after some new group has begun to show us once more *the* only way to paint. When one goes into a room full of pictures, one looks about for sensitiveness of vision, reality of conception, any kind of first-hand feeling.

Well, here may be seen some very competent painting of the French school, and a great deal that is not so competent; but the feeling which has stirred them all to the roots is the primordial mud-pie delight of dabbling about with lovely jammy paint. For the rest, there are many fairly good things, but few striking ones. Sickert gets thinner and thinner as he is spread out over a larger space. A skit which would be deliciously witty if it were three inches square;

or a good joke as an impromptu curtain for a charade, will *not* do when it is ten feet square, and in a serious exhibition. It is altogether too poor. Roger Fry is not so competent as many others, but he has a quality of sensitiveness which perhaps the others did not even wish to possess. They do all bang the notes so loud. Except Duncan Grant. His *Doorway* is brilliant. It is like champagne: effervescent and sparkling: whereas Mark Gertler's work may be described as having *great strength and grip,* like the advertisements of some brands of kitchen tea. Most of the others may be labelled *Latest Paris Fashions,* though they would no doubt prefer to be ticketed (like a hat I once saw) *Paris Anticipation.*

Edward Marsh was a senior civil servant, secretary to Winston Churchill, Rupert Brooke's executor and friend of Roger Fry and VB. His 1918 hagiography of Brooke which Virginia felt 'disgraceful soppy sentimental' was the beginning of his 'canonisation'.

52 Tavistock Sqre, WC1   3rd February 1931

My dear Gwen,

   What an age since we met! – I don't even know your address, & so must send this to the Keynes's. This is only a dull business letter, to ask if you think that anything could now be done – since Mrs Brooke is dead – about Rupert's letters. I came across a copy of some of those to you & Jacques that you sent me, & I rather think you said at the time that they must wait till Mrs Brooke was dead. It seems more & more idiotic that Eddy Marsh should be allowed to parade his hairdresser's block. Let me know if you think anything can be done. A vile and repulsive book about him by a man called, I think, Maurice Brown, an American, was sent us the other day. But we refused to touch it – not the beautiful Brown who wrote to me 2 or 3 years ago, but another, an actor I think.

   I suppose you're never in London & I suppose you're always busy, so I send this, instead of meeting.

   Is your new house nice, & the children, & painting & Cambridge & life altogether?

   Yours ever,

   Virginia

Lytton Strachey died on 22nd January 1932, a week after Virginia and Leonard visited him at Ham Spray. They returned on 10th March in an attempt to cheer up Carrington, but she shot herself the next day.

52 Tavistock Square, WC1   Sunday [1932]

Dear Gwen,

   I ought to have written before, but I've been in a rush. Yes do come – not this week; but what about next – Tuesday or Wednesday, 4.30 – (I think they're the 9th & 10th) Let me know if one of those would do; & come here if you will.

   Yours
   Virginia

I'm sure you understand what Lytton's death means to us.

FROM VIRGINIA WOOLF TO GWEN RAVERAT

This may be the last letter Virginia wrote Gwen.

Sunday [month and year unknown]

Dear Gwen,

Only a line to say I was so sorry to be so dull & stupid this evening when I had heaps of things I wanted to talk about but I was rather afflicted with the headache.

Come soon again, if you can bear it.

I am an affectionate, if intolerably stupid

old & faithful

Creature…

How are you? happy at all?

Thurso
Conduit Head Road
Cambridge   [undated – probably 1942]

Dear Leonard

Thank you for your letter – Will you please send Rupert's letters here; I had forgotten all about them – Thank you again.

I never wrote to you when Virginia died – chiefly because one gets to a state when there seems nothing at all to say about a thing like that – & partly because I've been working so hard for so long that I never manage to write any letters at all. But I *did – do* – mind her death – she was one of the people that have some how mattered in my life – & I know you will believe that you have my sympathy.

If ever there is talk of publishing her letters, there are a lot she wrote to Jacques, in 1924 or thereabouts, which I could lend.

Yrs ever
Gwen Raverat

Thurso
Conduit Head Road
Cambridge

Dear Leonard.

Thank you for your letter —
Will you please send Rupert's letters
here; I had forgotten all about
them — Thank you again.

I never wrote to you when
Virginia died — chiefly because
one gets to a stake when there
seems nothing at all to say
about a thing like that — or
partly because I've been
working so hard for so long that
I never manage to write
any letters at all. But I
did ——do—— mind her death

Feb 21
1983

The Old Granary,
Silver Street,
Cambridge.

Dear Leonard. I am touched &
honoured by your having taken the trouble
to write to me about my book; and
particularly by your saying that Virginia would
have liked it. There is nobody whose
opinions I should value more than yours &
hers. Thank you.
Yes, it is an age since we met. And
how awfully old we are all getting. But I
hope you are well. Yrs sincerely
Gwen Raverat

Started when she was 64, Gwen had no inkling that Period
Piece, *an idiosyncratic and charming memoir of her childhood,
would become a non-fiction best-seller. In the autumn of 1951,
at the age of 66, she only had a few more drawings to do for the
illustrations when she had a stroke that left her paralysed on her
left side. (The dramatic change in her handwriting evident in
the letters reproduced on the two previous pages was one of many
unwanted results.) The book was published on October 11th, 1952
and is still in print. It has sold many thousand copies and has
been translated into many languages.*
Gwen Raverat died on 11th February 1957.

The Old Granary
Silver Street
Cambridge   Feb 21, 1953

Dear Leonard,

   I am touched & honoured by your having taken the trouble to write to me about my book; and particularly by your
saying that Virginia would have liked it. There is nobody
whose opinions I should value more than yours and hers.
Thank you.

   Yes, it is an age since we met. And how awfully old we
are all getting. But I hope you are well.

   Yrs sincerely,
   Gwen Raverat

Acknowledgements

I am particularly grateful to my aunt, Elisabeth Hambro, who first compiled these letters; my mother, Sophie Gurney, who encouraged me from the beginning; my wife, Joy, who has been my scaffolding throughout; my cousins, Christian Hambro, for taking the time to research and scan pictures, and Felix Pryor, for his support, epistolary expertise and ear for a title; my oldest sister, Emily Hussey, for her translations; Humphrey Stone, for his patience and pursuit of the page beautiful; and for their encouragement and time: Rosemary Davidson of the Broughton House Gallery, Shelagh Boyd, Penny Stopa, Michael Mann and Henrietta Garnett.

I have leant heavily on the research and lucidity of several books (and, in some cases, on the generosity of their authors): Frances Spalding's superb biography of my grandmother: *Gwen Raverat: Friends Family and Affections*, Hermione Lee's poetic and never dull biography of Virginia Woolf; Reynolds Stone's (Humphrey Stone's father) *The Wood Engravings of Gwen Raverat*; Nigel Nicolson & Joanne Trautmann's editions of Virginia Woolf's letters; and Anne Bell's editions of Virginia Woolf's diaries.

I am also grateful for the kindness shown by the world of Woolfian studies in general, and in particular the organisers of the International Virginia Woolf Conference, for their tolerance and kindness to this bumbling iconoclast; David Scrace and Craig Hartley at the Fitzwilliam Museum, Cambridge; Dorothy Sheridan and Joy Eldridge at Sussex University Library; Adam Perkins at the Cambridge University Library; and Jeremy Crow at The Society of Authors.

The editor and publishers are grateful to the following for permission to quote materials in copyright: Random House, Harcourt Trade and Sussex University for the Virginia Woolf letters, diaries and journal; Elisabeth Hambro and Sophie Gurney for the Jacques and Gwen Raverat letters, writings, wood engravings, drawings and paintings; the Syndics of the Fitzwilliam Museum, Cambridge for the drawings and sketches by Gwen Raverat; the National Portrait Gallery for a photograph of Virginia Woolf, Hesperus Press for the entry from Virginia Woolf's journal.

Index

Villa Adèle: Raverats move to, 45

Willoughby de Broke, Lord, 100

Wilson, Steuart: the singer, at
Vence, 127

Woolf, Leonard: GR writes to, 196,
199; married, 40; his name, 47;
orders onions, 130; writes for the
Nation, 50

Woolf, Virginia: affair with Clive
Bell, 167; arranges visit to Vence,
50; bohemian, 18; deep affection
for JR, 15; famous, 101; gets news
of JR's death, 173; going to
Vence, 79; 'Gwen hearty direct
stodgy', 184; idealizes Raverats,
164; 'Its life that matters', 173;
Jacob's Room, 45, 49, 50, 104; her
journal, 16; madness, 52, 101, 181;
on 'loving one's own sex', 137;
Monday or Tuesday, 45, 49, 104;
Mrs Dalloway, 100; *Mrs Dalloway*
sent to Jacques, 18; *Night and Day*,
45; to print book by JR, 85; a
prude?, 110; railway line of a
sentence, 109; renewed corre-
spondence with JR, 17; on
sapphism, 17–18; and sending
proofs, 135; smokes Sir George's
cigar, 139; *The Common Reader*, 100;
The Voyage Out, 23, 33, 40, 45; visits
Cambridge, 91; wanted to buy a
Matisse, 58; wants something of
Jacques's, 181; writes from
Madrid, 57
**extracts from her diaries &
journal**, 23, 116, 173, 184
letters: to Dorothy Bussy, 121; to
GR, 40, 160, 167, 169, 180, 190, 193,
194, 195; to JR, 33, 35, 45, 50, 57, 63,
76, 83, 90, 98, 109, 123, 129, 135, 144;
to VB, 36